# ANARCHISM, REVOLUTION, AND TERRORISM

# ANARCHISM, REVOLUTION, AND TERRORISM

Edited by Nicholas Croce

Britannica®
Educational Publishing

IN ASSOCIATION WITH

ROSEN
EDUCATIONAL SERVICES

Published in 2015 by Britannica Educational Publishing (a trademark of Encyclopædia Britannica, Inc.) in association with The Rosen Publishing Group, Inc.
29 East 21st Street, New York, NY 10010

Distributed exclusively by Rosen Publishing.
To see additional Britannica Educational Publishing titles, go to rosenpublishing.com.

First Edition

**Britannica Educational Publishing**
J.E. Luebering: Director, Core Reference Group
Anthony L. Green: Editor, Compton's by Britannica

**Rosen Publishing**
Hope Lourie Killcoyne: Executive Editor
Nicholas Croce: Editor
Nelson Sá: Art Director
Brian Garvey: Designer
Cindy Reiman: Photography Manager
Amy Feinberg: Photo Researcher

### Cataloging-in-Publication Data

Anarchism, revolution, and terrorism/edited by Nicholas Croce.—First edition.
    pages cm.—(Political and economic systems)
Includes bibliographical references and index.
ISBN 978-1-62275-353-6 (library bound)
1. Anarchism—History—Juvenile literature. 2. Revolutions—History—Juvenile literature. 3. Terrorism—History—Juvenile literature. I. Croce, Nicholas.
HX826.A48 2015
335'.83—dc23
                                 2014004687

*Manufactured in the United States of America*

**On the cover, p. 3:** *Words/Shutterstock.com*

# CONTENTS

52

63

# INTRODUCTION

Hidden gunmen fire on a group of unsuspecting soldiers. Are they terrorists, or are they freedom fighters? After all, that situation could describe American soldiers being ambushed in Afghanistan, but it could also describe tactics Americans used in the Revolutionary War. How a person feels about those tactics depends on whether one is on the side that is in control or on the side seeking to disrupt that control.

There have always been those who have rebelled against the ruling order. To a large extent, the history of nations has been a long-running debate over the best form of government. Democracy, communism, monarchy, fascism—these and others have all been tried, and each has its advocates. Each form of government also has its detractors, either in terms of ideology or in how the system is implemented. As a result, throughout history and around the globe, there have been people intent on overthrowing their governments.

Just as there are different approaches to governing, there are different approaches to rejecting the existing government. Anarchy, open revolution, and terrorism are examples of these approaches. All are expressions of extreme dissatisfaction with the status quo, and as such, each has played a disruptive role in history. This book looks at the theories behind anarchy, revolution, and terrorism and highlights several dramatic examples of how they have been applied.

While rebels often seek to replace one system of government with another, what if a person does not believe in government at all? The desire to eliminate government altogether is known as anarchism. The word "anarchy" is derived from the Greek, meaning "without authority." Anarchists believe that nobody has the moral authority to create laws that govern

*Occupy Wall Street protesters march through downtown Los Angeles, Calif., on Oct. 3, 2011.* Frederic J. Brown/AFP/Getty Images

others and that property ownership is simply a means of someone stealing for themselves what should rightly belong to all.

Though one of the earliest advocates of anarchism, 19th century French philosopher Pierre-Joseph Proudhon, favoured peaceful changes to society, anarchism quickly became associated with more radical thinkers and more violent tactics. The use of dramatic, violent acts to publicize the cause of anarchy was known as "propaganda of the deed" and came to characterize the anarchist movement in the late 19th and early 20th centuries. Often these acts of violence seemed so cruel and indiscriminate that they turned public opinion against anarchy.

Still, anarchy was far from a fringe concept. Anarchy's distrust of centralized government was also one of the principles of federalism, which influenced the United States Constitution. To an even greater degree, anarchism shared a number of characteristics with communism. Over the years, anarchism would develop a complex and often contentious relationship with communism.

Both anarchism and communism rely on the principle of collectivism, which is the belief that property and effort should be shared for the common good of society. The key difference, though, is that anarchists believe this sharing should be practiced voluntarily by local organizations, while communists believe it must be imposed on the people by a central authority.

Anarchism and communism also shared a close relationship with various workers' movements of the late 19th and early 20th centuries. An influential segment of unions in many countries came to believe in syndicalism, which was the elimination of capitalism in favour of control by the workers. This rejection of private ownership in favour of collective benefit from economic production gave anarchism a significant following among unions in the early 20th century.

Fueled largely by its association with unions, anarchism became a prominent dissident force in many parts of Europe, Asia, and the Americas. In particular, anarchism took root in Spain, where militant anarchists dominated the National Confederation of Labour, an organization that grew to include two million members. During the early stages of the Spanish Civil War in the 1930s, anarchist groups were even able to control large sections of eastern Spain.

As anarchism gained followers, several high-profile violent acts were committed in the name of the movement. These included the murders of the king of Italy, the president of France, the prime minister of Spain, and in the United States, the assassination of Pres. William McKinley in 1901.

In addition to violence, economic protest by syndicalists under the influence of anarchists took the form of general strikes in a number of European countries in the early 1900s. A general strike is one that cuts across multiple industries and thus is particularly damaging economically. In the second half of the 20th century, anarchism was an influence in the use of civil disobedience by the American civil rights movement, and it was also a factor in the radical student movements around the world in the 1960s. Even more recently, elements of anarchism could be seen in widely publicized protests such as the demonstrations against a meeting of the World Trade Organization in Seattle and in the Occupy Wall Street movement, which followed the 2008 financial crisis.

Despite developing a global following and inspiring some prominent actions, the global influence of anarchism had largely faded by the mid-1900s. The success of the communist revolution in Russia led many to turn to communism rather than anarchism as an alternative to capitalism. For others, the gains made by the union movement on behalf of workers made them more content to remain within a capitalist system.

Ultimately though, anarchism's fatal flaw might be one of its main principles—decentralization. Any movement that does not believe in a strong, central organization almost inevitably will have trouble sustaining momentum toward coherent goals. Still, as long as governments have flaws—and all do—the idea of eliminating centralized government will appeal to some.

Whereas anarchy seeks to abolish centralized government, revolutions generally aim to replace one governing authority with another. Revolutions have played a prominent role in the history of several major nations, and the frequency of revolutions has accelerated in recent centuries.

The intellectual roots of revolution grew out of the rise of secular humanism during the Renaissance and thereafter. Previously, people generally accepted that the established order of things was the will of God. However, as secular humanism began to establish the right—or even responsibility—of societies to determine their own destinies, people increasingly began to question their leaders, and they looked to revolution as a means of addressing inequities.

Nineteenth-century social theorist Karl Marx represented the culmination of this growing tendency to question the established order, and he became an extremely influential revolutionary figure. Marx believed that human history went through a series of natural stages and that the ultimate stage was one in which the working class overthrew the property-owning class. He believed that the proletariat, or the broad class of labourers, had to control the means of economic production in order for a society to truly advance.

At a time when mass populations of labourers struggled under brutal working conditions for minimal compensation, Marxist theories garnered a broad base of public appeal. The 20th century would see Marxist revolutions take control in countries such as Russia, China, Cuba, Vietnam, and Yugoslavia.

While Marxism became a frequent goal for which revolutions were fought, many revolutions were driven as much by what they were fighting against as what they were fighting for. In many cases, such as in America and Haiti, revolutions were fought to shake off oppression by colonial rulers. In cases such as the French and Turkish revolutions, people sought to overthrow narrow, autocratic rule in favour of broader representation. This was also a factor in the Arab Spring revolts in Tunisia, Egypt, and Libya. Religion also played a role in the Arab Spring, just as it had in revolutions as widely separated by time and distance as England's overthrow of King James II and the Iranian Revolution of 1978–79.

Of course, overthrowing a country's leaders is easier said than done. Revolutionaries do not typically have ready-made armies at their disposal, and so they have to start with a series of small, stealthy actions and build momentum from there. This is why guerrilla warfare and terrorism have become important tools in achieving revolutionary goals.

Guerrilla warfare is the use of fast-moving, unconventional military strikes by forces that can then quickly find concealment in the countryside or by blending in with the general population. Tactics include organization into small units for flexibility and secrecy, the use of improvised weapons, reliance on the land or a sympathetic populace for sustenance, and the use of harassment to wear down an enemy rather than trying to defeat a superior force in major head-to-head conflicts.

The success of a guerrilla campaign depends heavily on the support of the public. Unless guerrilla forces can tap into the resentments and aspirations of a country's population, they will lack economic support, their secrecy will be compromised, and their pool of new recruits will dry up. For this reason, propaganda can be an essential nonmilitary component of guerrilla warfare because it can convince a significant segment of the population that the guerrillas are fighting for their benefit.

Guerrilla warfare played a role in America's Revolutionary War and in the Duke of Wellington's defeat of Napoleon. It was a leading tactic of T.E. Lawrence—popularly known as Lawrence of Arabia—in World War I and of the Irish Republican Army. It was used with great success by the North Vietnamese in the Vietnam War, and it was deployed by Afghan rebels first against a Soviet-backed regime in the 1980s and more recently against the U.S.-backed regime that followed the overthrow of the Taliban. Whenever there is a need for a rebel force to overcome superior military odds, guerrilla warfare will be a likely strategy.

If guerrilla warfare is a way of levelling the playing field militarily, terrorism is a tactic that seeks to make the battle completely one-sided by striking against unsuspecting and often unarmed targets. Its intent is psychological, to strike fear not just in the victims but in society in general. The goal is to bring about some form of political objective, which can range from changing a particular government policy to ousting an occupying force or overthrowing a regime. Thus, it can be part of a revolutionary campaign, but it can also be used to accomplish narrower goals.

Terrorist tactics include kidnappings, hijackings, hostage taking, car bombings, and suicide bombings. Terrorism has been practiced by a great many groups over the years, including the Ku Klux Klan in America's post–Civil War South, radical leftists such as the Red Brigades in Italy and the Baader-Meinhof Gang in Germany, the Irish Republican Army in strikes against the British and against rivals in their own country, and by Islamist extremists in the Middle East.

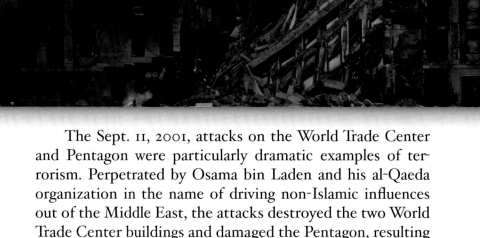

*Fire and smoke billow from the Pentagon in Arlington County, Va., after hijackers crashed American Airlines Flight 77 into the building during the Sept. 11, 2001, terrorist attacks.* Cpl. Jason Ingersoll, USMC/U.S. Department of Defense

The Sept. 11, 2001, attacks on the World Trade Center and Pentagon were particularly dramatic examples of terrorism. Perpetrated by Osama bin Laden and his al-Qaeda organization in the name of driving non-Islamic influences out of the Middle East, the attacks destroyed the two World Trade Center buildings and damaged the Pentagon, resulting in the loss of thousands of lives. By inflicting such damage and bringing the Middle East conflict to America's shores, the September 11 attacks raised the fear of terrorism to an unprecedented degree.

In this sense, the September 11 attacks succeeded in causing widespread fear and long-lasting disruption. However, they not only failed to accomplish their stated objective, but they may have been counterproductive to that cause. Worldwide sympathies after the attack were overwhelmingly in favour of the victims rather than the attackers, and the resulting reprisals cost al-Qaeda its primary base of operations and many of its leaders, including ultimately bin Laden. Whereas guerrilla warfare can point to some historic successes in accomplishing its goals, terrorist acts like those of September 11 often just seem like a violent lashing out rather than a pragmatic means to an end.

By definition, anarchism, revolution, and terrorism are actions against a prevailing authority, and thus they tend to vary with the situation rather than exhibit uniform characteristics. Still, there are recurring themes in all these approaches, and a central one is that they seek to effect radical changes. By examining several examples of anarchism, revolution, and terrorism, this book will illustrate the various tactics and motivations that have surrounded this type of desire for systemic change. Those examples, in turn, will help the reader get a sense of why these methods are so frequently condemned, but also why disenchanted people around the world have so frequently turned to these approaches.

# CHAPTER 1

# ANARCHISM

Anarchism is a cluster of doctrines and attitudes centred on the belief that government is both harmful and unnecessary. Anarchist thought developed in the West and spread throughout the world, principally in the early 20th century.

Derived from the Greek root *anarchos*, meaning "without authority," the terms "anarchism," "anarchist," and "anarchy" are used to express both approval and disapproval. In early usage all these terms were pejorative: for example, during the English Civil Wars (1642–51) the radical Levellers, who called for universal manhood suffrage, were referred to by their opponents as "Switzerising anarchists," and during the French Revolution the leader of the moderate Girondin faction of Parliament, Jacques-Pierre Brissot, accused his most extreme rivals, the Enragés, of being the advocates of "anarchy":

*Laws that are not carried into effect, authorities without force and despised, crime unpunished, property attacked, the safety of the individual violated, the morality of the people corrupted, no constitution, no government, no justice, these are the features of anarchy.*

These words could serve as a model for the denunciations delivered by all opponents of anarchism. The anarchists, for their part, would admit many of Brissot's points. They deny man-made laws, regard property as a means of tyranny, and believe that crime is merely the product of property and authority. But they would argue that their denial of constitutions and governments leads not to "no justice" but to the real justice inherent in the free development of man's sociality—his natural inclination, when unfettered by laws, to live according to the principles and practice of mutual aid.

# Foundations of Anarchist Thought

The first person willingly to call himself an anarchist was the French political writer and pioneer socialist Pierre-Joseph Proudhon (Jan. 15, 1809–Jan. 19, 1865). In his controversial study of the economic bases of society, *Qu'est ce que la propriété?* (1840; *What Is Property?*), Proudhon argued that the real laws of society have nothing to do with authority but rather stem from the nature of society itself, and he foresaw the eventual dissolution of authority and the emergence of a natural social order: "As man seeks justice in equality, so society seeks order in anarchy. Anarchy—the absence of a sovereign—such is the form of government to which we are every day approximating."

The essential elements of Proudhon's philosophy already had been developed by earlier thinkers. The rejection of political authority has a rich pedigree. It extends back to classical antiquity—to the Stoics and the Cynics—and runs through the Middle Ages and the Renaissance, as illustrated by dissenting Christian sects such as the medieval Catharists and certain factions of Anabaptists. For such groups—which are often mistakenly claimed as ancestors by modern anarchist writers—the rejection of government was merely one aspect of a retreat from the material world into a realm of spiritual grace, and as part of the search for individual salvation it

*Oil painting of Pierre-Joseph Proudhon, 1865*. Imagno/Hulton Fine Art Collection/Getty Images

was hardly compatible with the sociopolitical doctrine of anarchism. In all its forms, that doctrine consists of (1) an analysis of the power relations underlying existing forms of political authority and (2) a vision of an alternative libertarian society based on cooperation, as opposed to competition and coercion, and functioning without the need for government authority.

# English Anarchist Thought

The first sketch of an anarchist commonwealth in this sense was developed in England in the years immediately following the English Civil Wars (1642–51) by Gerrard Winstanley, a dissenting Christian and founder of the Digger movement. In his pamphlet of 1649, *Truth Lifting Up Its Head Above Scandals*, Winstanley laid down what later became basic principles among anarchists: that power corrupts; that property is incompatible with freedom; that authority and property are between them the begetters of crime; and that only in a society without rulers, where work and its products are shared, can men be free and happy, acting not according to laws imposed from above but according to their consciences. Winstanley was not only the pioneer theorist of anarchism but also the forerunner of anarchist activism. In 1649, calling upon the people "to manure and work upon the common lands," he and a band of followers occupied a hillside in southern England and established a society of agrarian free communism.

The Digger experiment was destroyed by local landowners, and Winstanley vanished into such obscurity that the place and date of his death are unknown. But the principles he defended lingered on in the traditions of English Protestant sects and reached their ultimate flowering in the work of a former dissenting minister, William Godwin. In his masterpiece, *Political Justice* (1793), Godwin not only presents the classic anarchist argument that authority is against nature and that social evils exist because men are not free to act according to reason, he also sketches out a decentralized society composed of small autonomous communities, or parishes. Within these communities democratic political procedures would be dispensed with as far as possible because, according to Godwin, they encourage a majoritarian tyranny and dilute individual responsibility. Godwin also condemns "accumulated property" as a source of power over others and envisions a loose economic system in which people would give and take according to their needs. Godwin was a prophet of technological progress, and he believed that industrial development would eventually reduce the necessary working time to half an hour a day, provided people lived simply, and that this arrangement would facilitate the transition to a society without authority.

Godwin enjoyed great celebrity in the 1790s and influenced varied writers such as Percy Bysshe Shelley (whose *Queen Mab* and *Prometheus Unbound* are virtually anarchist poems), William Wordsworth, William Hazlitt, and Robert Owen. By the time of his death in 1836, however, he was almost forgotten. Although his ideas had a subterranean influence on the British labour movement through the work of Owen, they had virtually no effect on the quasi-political anarchist movement on the continent of Europe during the mid-19th century.

# Pierre-Joseph Proudhon and French Anarchist Thought

Pierre-Joseph Proudhon was a French libertarian socialist and journalist whose doctrines became the basis for later radical and anarchist theory.

Proudhon was born into poverty as the son of a feckless cooper and tavern keeper, and at the age of nine he worked as

# William Godwin

William Godwin (March 3, 1756–April 7, 1836) was a social philosopher, political journalist, and religious dissenter who anticipated the English Romantic literary movement with his writings advancing atheism, anarchism, and personal freedom.

Godwin's idealistic liberalism was based on the principle of the absolute sovereignty and competence of reason to determine right choice. An optimist regarding man's future perfectibility, he combined cultural determinism with a doctrine of extreme individualism. The object of his principal work, *An Enquiry Concerning Political Justice, and Its Influence on General Virtue and Happiness* (1793), was to reject conventional government by demonstrating the corrupting evil and tyranny inherent in its power of manipulation. He proposed in its place small self-subsisting communities. He argued that social institutions fail because they impose on man generalized thought categories and preconceived ideas, which make it impossible to see things as they are.

It has been claimed that Godwin's works laid the foundations for the mutually contradictory doctrines of communism and anarchy. In fact their germ, though undeveloped, is to be found in two separate elements in his thinking. He advocated neither the abolition nor the "communalization" of property; property was to be held, a sacred trust, at the disposal of him whose need was greatest. His most powerful personal belief was that "everything understood by the term co-operation is in some sense an evil," from which proceeded his most influential anarchic doctrines.

Among his other writings are *The Enquirer* (1797), a collection of essays; *Of Population* (1820), a reply to Thomas Malthus's writings on the subject; *Thoughts on Man: His Nature, Production, and Discoveries* (1831); and his widely acclaimed ideological novel, *Things as They Are; or, The Adventures of Caleb Williams* (1794).

Godwin was married in 1797 to Mary Wollstonecraft, who was the mother of his daughter Mary Wollstonecraft Shelley.

a cowherd in the Jura Mountains. Proudhon's country childhood and peasant ancestry influenced his ideas to the end of his life, and his vision of the ideal society almost to the end remained that of a world in which peasant farmers and small craftsmen like his father could live in freedom, peace, and dignified poverty, for luxury repelled him, and he never sought it for himself or others.

Proudhon at an early age showed signs of intellectual brilliance, and he won a scholarship to the college at Besançon. Despite the humiliation of being a child in *sabots* (wooden shoes) among the sons of merchants, he developed a taste for learning and retained it even when his family's financial disasters forced him to become an apprentice printer and later a compositor. While he learned his craft, he taught himself Latin, Greek, and Hebrew, and in the printing shop he not only conversed with various local liberals and Socialists but also met and fell under the influence of a fellow citizen of Besançon, the utopian socialist Charles Fourier.

With other young printers, Proudhon later attempted to establish his own press, but bad management destroyed the venture, and it may well have been compounded by his own growing interest in writing, which led him to develop a French prose style difficult to translate but admired by writers as varied as Flaubert, Sainte-Beuve, and Baudelaire. Eventually, in 1838, a scholarship awarded by the Besançon Academy enabled him to study in Paris. Now, with leisure to formulate his ideas, he wrote his first significant book, *Qu'est-ce que la propriété?* (1840; *What Is Property?*, 1876). This created a sensation, for Proudhon not only declared, "I am an anarchist"; he also stated, "Property is theft!"

This slogan, which gained much notoriety, was an example of Proudhon's inclination to attract attention and mask the true nature of his thought by inventing striking phrases. He did not attack property in the generally accepted

*Karl Marx.* Roger Viollet/Getty Images

sense but only the kind of property by which one man exploits the labour of another. Property in another sense—in the right of the farmer to possess the land he works and the craftsman his workshop and tools—he regarded as essential for the preservation of liberty, and his principal criticism of communism, whether of the utopian or the Marxist variety, was that it destroyed freedom by taking away from the individual control over his means of production.

In the somewhat reactionary atmosphere of the July monarchy in the 1840s, Proudhon narrowly missed prosecution for his statements in *What Is Property?*; and he was brought into court when, in 1842, he published a more inflammatory sequel, *Avertissement aux propriétaires* (*Warning to Proprietors*, 1876). In this first of his trials, Proudhon escaped conviction because the jury conscientiously found that they could not clearly understand his arguments and therefore could not condemn them.

In 1843 he went to Lyon to work as managing clerk in a water transport firm. There he encountered a weavers' secret society, the Mutualists, who had evolved a protoanarchist doctrine that taught that the factories of the dawning industrial age could be operated by associations of workers and that these workers, by economic action rather than by violent revolution, could transform society. Such views were at variance with the Jacobin revolutionary tradition in France, with its stress on political centralism. Nevertheless, Proudhon accepted their views and later paid tribute to his Lyonnais working-class mentors by adopting the name of Mutualism for his own form of anarchism.

As well as encountering the obscure working-class theoreticians of Lyon, Proudhon also met the feminist socialist Flora Tristan and, on his visits to Paris, made the acquaintance of Karl Marx, Mikhail Bakunin, and the Russian socialist and writer Aleksandr Herzen. In 1846 he took issue with Marx over the organization of the socialist movement, objecting to Marx's authoritarian and centralist ideas. Shortly afterward, when Proudhon published his *Système des contradictions économiques, ou Philosophie de la misère* (1846; *System of Economic Contradictions: or, The Philosophy of Poverty*, 1888), Marx attacked him bitterly in a book-length polemic *La misère de la philosophie* (1847; *The Poverty of Philosophy*, 1910). It was the beginning of a historic rift between libertarian and authoritarian socialists and between anarchists and Marxists that, after Proudhon's death, was to rend socialism's First International apart in the feud between Marx and Proudhon's disciple Bakunin and which has lasted to this day.

Early in 1848 Proudhon abandoned his post in Lyon and went to Paris, where in February he started the paper *Le Représentant du peuple*. During the revolutionary year of 1848 and the first months of 1849 he edited a total of four papers; the earliest were more or less regular anarchist periodicals and all of them were destroyed in turn by government censorship. Proudhon himself took a minor part in the Revolution of 1848, which he regarded as devoid of any sound theoretical basis. Though he was elected to the Constituent Assembly of the Second Republic in June 1848, he confined himself mainly to criticizing the authoritarian tendencies that were emerging in the revolution and that led up to the dictatorship of Napoleon III. Proudhon also attempted unsuccessfully to establish a People's Bank based on mutual credit and labour checks, which paid the worker according to the time expended on his product. He was eventually imprisoned in 1849 for criticizing Louis-Napoleon, who had become president of the republic prior to declaring himself Emperor Napoleon III, and Proudhon was not released until 1852.

His conditions of imprisonment were—by 20th-century standards—light. His friends could visit him, and he was allowed to go out occasionally in Paris. He married and begat his first child while he was imprisoned. From his cell he also edited the last issues of his last paper (with the financial assistance of Herzen) and wrote two of his most important books, the never translated *Confessions d'un révolutionnaire* (1849) and *Idée générale de la révolution au XIXe siècle* (1851; *The General Idea of the Revolution in the Nineteenth Century*, 1923). The latter—in its portrait of a federal world society with frontiers abolished, national states eliminated, and authority decentralized among communes or locality associations, and with free contracts replacing laws—presents perhaps more completely than any other of Proudhon's works the vision of his ideal society.

After Proudhon's release from prison in 1852 he was constantly harassed by the imperial police; he found it impossible to publish his writings and supported himself by preparing anonymous guides for investors and other similar hack works. When, in 1858, he persuaded a publisher to bring out his three-volume masterpiece *De la justice dans la Révolution et dans l'église*, in which he opposed a humanist theory of justice to the church's transcendental assumptions, his book was seized. Having fled to Belgium, he was sentenced in absentia to further imprisonment. He remained in exile until 1862, developing his criticisms of nationalism and his ideas of world federation (embodied in *Du Principe fédératif*, 1863).

On his return to Paris, Proudhon began to gain influence among the workers; Paris craftsmen who had adopted his Mutualist ideas were among the founders of the First International just before his death in 1865. His last work, completed on his death bed, *De la capacité politique des classes ouvrières* (1865), developed the theory that the liberation of the workers must be their own task, through economic action.

Proudhon was not the first to enunciate the doctrine that is now called anarchism; before he claimed it, it had already been sketched out by, among others, the English philosopher

William Godwin in prose and his follower Percy Bysshe Shelley in verse.

There is no evidence, however, that Proudhon ever studied the works of either Godwin or Shelley, and his characteristic doctrines of anarchism (society without government), Mutualism (workers' association for the purpose of credit banking), and federalism (the denial of centralized political organization) seem to have resulted from an original reinterpretation of French revolutionary thought modified by personal experience.

Proudhon was a solitary thinker who refused to admit that he had created a system and abhorred the idea of founding a party. There was thus something ironical about the breadth of influence that his ideas later developed. They were important in the First International and later became the basis of anarchist theory as developed by Mikhail Bakunin (who once remarked that "Proudhon was the master of us all") and the anarchist writer Peter Kropotkin. His concepts were influential among such varied groups as the Russian populists, the radical Italian nationalists of the 1860s, the Spanish federalists of the 1870s, and the syndicalist movement that developed in France and later became powerful in Italy and Spain. Until the beginning of the 1920s, Proudhon remained the most important single influence on French working-class radicalism, while in a more diffuse manner his ideas of decentralization and his criticisms of government had revived in the later 20th century, even though at times their origin was not recognized.

## Revolutionary Syndicalism

In France, where individualist trends had been most pronounced and public reaction to terrorist acts had imperiled the very existence of the movement, anarchists made an effort to acquire a mass following, primarily by infiltrating the trade unions. They were particularly active in the *bourses du travail* ("labour exchanges"), local groups of unions originally established to find work for their members. In 1892 a national confederation of *bourses du travail* was formed, and by 1895 a group of anarchists, led by Fernand Pelloutier, Émile Pouget, and Paul Delesalle, had gained effective control of the organization and were developing the theory and practice of working-class activism later known as anarcho-syndicalism, or revolutionary syndicalism.

The anarcho-syndicalists argued that the traditional function of trade unions—to struggle for better wages and working conditions—was not enough. The unions should become militant organizations dedicated to the destruction of capitalism and the state. They should aim to take over factories and utilities, which would then be operated by the workers. In this way the union or syndicate would have a double function—as an organ of struggle within the existing political system and as an organ of administration after the revolution. The anarcho-syndicalists' strategy called for sustaining militancy by creating an atmosphere of incessant conflict, which would culminate in a massive general strike. Many anarcho-syndicalists believed that such an overwhelming act of noncooperation would bring about what they called "the revolution of folded arms," resulting in the collapse of the state and the capitalist system. However, although partial general strikes, with limited objectives, were undertaken in France and elsewhere with varying success, the millennial general strike aimed at overthrowing the social order in a single blow was never attempted. Nevertheless, the anarcho-syndicalists acquired great prestige among the workers of France—and later of Spain and Italy—because of their generally tough-minded attitude at a time when working conditions were bad and employers tended to respond brutally to union activity. After the General Confederation of Labour (Confédération Générale du Travail; CGT), the great French trade-union organization, was founded in 1902, the militancy of the anarcho-syndicalists enabled them to retain control of the organization until 1908 and to wield considerable influence on its activities until after World War I.

Like anarchism, revolutionary syndicalism proved attractive to certain intellectuals, notably Georges Sorel, whose *Reflections on Violence* (1908) was the most important literary work to emerge from the movement. The more purist anarchist theoreticians were disturbed by the monolithic character of syndicalist organizations, which they feared might create powerful interest structures in a revolutionary society. At the International Anarchist Congress in Amsterdam in 1907 a crucial debate on this issue took place between the young revolutionary syndicalist Pierre Monatte and the veteran anarchist Errico Malatesta. It defined a division of outlook that still lingers in anarchist circles, which have always included individualist attitudes too extreme to admit any kind of large-scale organization.

Revolutionary syndicalism transformed anarchism, for a time at least, from a tiny minority current into a movement with considerable mass support, even though most members of syndicalist unions were sympathizers and fellow travelers rather than committed anarchists. In 1922 the syndicalists set up their own International with its headquarters in Berlin, taking the historic name of the International Workingmen's Association. When it was established, the organizations that formed it could still boast a considerable following. The Italian Trade Union (Unione Sindicale Italiana) had 500,000 members; the Regional Federation of Argentine Workers (Federación Obrera Regional Argentina), 200,000 members; the General Confederation of Labour (Confederação General de Trabalho) in Portugal,

150,000 members; and the Free Workers (Freie Arbeiter) in Germany, 120,000 members. There were also smaller organizations in Chile, Uruguay, Denmark, Norway, Holland, Mexico, and Sweden. In Britain, the influence of syndicalism was shown most clearly in the Guild Socialism movement, which flourished briefly in the early years of the 20th century. In the United States, revolutionary syndicalist ideas were influential in the Industrial Workers of the World (IWW), which in the years immediately before and after World War I played a vital part in organizing American miners, loggers, and unskilled workers. Only a small minority of IWW militants were avowed anarchists, however.

## Russian Anarchist Thought

Mikhail Bakunin (May 30 [May 18, Old Style], 1814–July 1 [June 19], 1876) had been a supporter of nationalist revolutionary movements in various Slav countries. In the 1840s he had come under the influence of Proudhon, and by the 1860s, when he entered the International, he had not only founded his own proto-anarchist organization— the Social Democratic Alliance, which had a considerable following in Italy, Spain, Switzerland, and the Rhône valley of France—but had modified Proudhonian teachings into a doctrine later known as collectivism. Bakunin accepted Proudhon's federalism and his insistence on the need for working-class direct action, but he argued that the modified property rights Proudhon allowed were impractical. Instead, he suggested that the means of production should be owned collectively, though he still held that each worker should be remunerated only according to the amount of work he actually performed. The second important difference between Bakunin and Proudhon lay in their concepts of revolutionary method. Proudhon believed it was possible to

*Late-1930s photograph of Republicans fighting against nationalist rebels during the Spanish Civil War.* AFP/Getty Images

create within existing society the mutualist associations that could replace it; he therefore opposed violent revolutionary action. Bakunin, declaring that "the passion for destruction is also a creative urge," refused to accept a piecemeal approach; a violent revolution, sweeping away all existing institutions, was in his view the necessary prelude to the construction of a free and peaceful society.

Although the individualism and nonviolence implicit in Proudhon's vision have survived in peripheral currents of the anarchist tradition, Bakunin's stress on collectivism and violent revolutionary action dominated mainstream anarchism from the days of the First International down to the destruction of anarchism as a mass movement at the end of the Spanish Civil War in 1939.

The First International was itself destroyed by the conflict between Marx and Bakunin, a conflict rooted as much in the contradictory personalities of the two leaders as in their rival doctrines—revolution by a disciplined party versus revolution by the spontaneous insurgence of the working class, respectively. When the International finally broke apart at the Hague congress in 1872, Bakunin's followers were left in control of the working-class movements in the Latin countries—Spain, Italy, southern France, and French-speaking Switzerland—and these movements were to remain the principal bases of anarchism in Europe. In 1873 the Bakuninists set up their own International, which lasted as an active body until 1877; during this period its members finally accepted the name anarchist rather than Mutualist.

Bakunin died in 1876. His ideas had been developed in action as well as in writing, for he was the hero of many barricades, prisons, and meetings. His successor as ideological leader was Peter Kropotkin, who had renounced the title of prince when he became a revolutionary in 1872. Kropotkin is more celebrated for his writing than for his actions, though in his early years he led an eventful career as a revolutionary militant, which he described in a fine autobiography, *Memoirs of a Revolutionist* (1899). Under the influence of Russian revolutionary populist thought as well as a comrade such as the French geographer Élisée Reclus (a former disciple of the French utopian socialist Charles Fourier), Kropotkin developed a variant of anarchist theory known as anarchist communism. Kropotkin and his followers went beyond Bakunin's collectivism, arguing not only that the means of production should be owned cooperatively but that there should be complete communism in terms of distribution. This theory revived the scheme described in Sir Thomas More's *Utopia* (1516), involving common storehouses from which everyone would be allowed to take whatever he wished on the basis of the formula "From each according to his means, to each according to his needs." In *The Conquest of Bread* (1892), Kropotkin sketched a vision of a revolutionary society organized as a federation of free communist groups. He reinforced this vision in *Mutual Aid: A Factor in Evolution* (1902), where he used biological and sociological evidence to argue that cooperation is more natural and usual than competition among both animals and human beings. In his *Fields, Factories, and Workshops* (1899) he developed ideas on the decentralization of industry appropriate to a nongovernmental society.

# Anarchism as a Movement, 1870–1940

A crucial development in the history of anarchism was the emergence of the doctrine of "propaganda of the deed." In 1876 Errico Malatesta expressed the belief held by Italian anarchists that "the insurrectionary deed destined to affirm socialist principles by acts, is the most efficacious means of propaganda." The first acts were rural insurrections intended to arouse the illiterate masses of the Italian countryside. After the insurrections failed, anarchist activism tended to take the form of acts of terrorism by individual protesters, who would attempt to kill ruling figures to make the state appear vulnerable and to inspire the masses with their self-sacrifice. Between 1890 and 1901 several such symbolic murders were carried out; the victims included King Umberto I of Italy, the empress consort Elizabeth of Austria, Pres. Sadi Carnot of France, Pres. William McKinley of the United States, and Antonio Cánovas del Castillo, the prime minister of Spain. This dramatic series of terrorist acts established the image of the anarchist as a mindless destroyer, an image that was further strengthened as anarchist attacks on government officials, as well as on restaurants and other public places, became more widespread.

During the 1890s, especially in France, anarchism was adopted as a philosophy by many avant-garde artistic and literary figures, including the painters Gustave Courbet (who had been a disciple of Proudhon), Camille Pissarro, Georges Seurat, and Paul Signac and the writers Paul Adam, Octave Mirbeau, Laurent Tailhade, and Felix Fénéon. The Symbolist poet Stéphane Mallarmé was also a strong sympathizer. In England, the Irish poet and dramatist Oscar Wilde declared himself an anarchist and, under Kropotkin's inspiration, wrote the essay "The Soul of Man Under Socialism" (1891).

Artists were attracted by the individualist spirit of anarchism. By the mid-1890s, however, the more militant anarchists in France began to realize that an excess of individualism had detached them from the workers they sought to liberate. Anarchists, indeed, have always found it difficult to reconcile the claims of general human solidarity with the demands—equally insistent—of the individual who desires freedom. Some anarchist thinkers, such as the German Max Stirner, refused to recognize any limitation on the individual's right to do as he pleases or any obligation to act socially; and even those who accepted Kropotkin's socially oriented doctrines of anarchist communism have in practice been reluctant to create forms of organization that threatened their freedom of action or seemed likely to harden into institutions.

In consequence, although a number of international anarchist congresses were held—the most celebrated being those in London in 1881 and Amsterdam in 1907—no effective worldwide organization was ever created, even though by the end of the 19th century the anarchist movement had spread to all continents and was united by informal links of correspondence and friendship between leading figures. National federations were weak even in countries where there were many anarchists, such as France and Italy, and the

# Errico Malatesta

Errico (also spelled Enrico) Malatesta (Dec. 14, 1853–July 22, 1932) was an Italian anarchist and agitator, a leading advocate of "propaganda of the deed," the doctrine urged largely by Italian anarchists that revolutionary ideas could best be spread by armed insurrection.

Malatesta became politically active while still in his teens, joining the First International in 1871. A dynamic speaker and propagandist, he soon became a leader in the anarchist movement and helped organize anarchist revolutionary groups in Romania, Italy, Spain, and elsewhere in Europe, in Egypt, and in North and South America, including Argentina. Imprisoned for a total of about 12 years during his long career, he was sentenced to death three times and spent some 35 years in exile. Though often associated with the Russian anarchist Peter Kropotkin, Malatesta laid more emphasis on the organization of revolutionaries and workers as a means of achieving anarchist political goals. Accordingly, he helped organize workers' congresses in France, Belgium, and Switzerland at which he urged armed revolt, and subsequently he was banished from each of those countries.

In 1899 he visited the United States, lecturing and editing an anarchist journal. After 1900 he lived more or less quietly in London for many years, taking time out to agitate for revolution in Italy in 1913–14. He returned permanently to Italy after an amnesty in 1919, engaging in political activity until the fascists' rise to power in 1922.

typical unit of organization remained the small group dedicated to propaganda by deed or word. Such groups engaged in a wide variety of activities; in the 1890s many of them set up experimental schools and communities in an attempt to live according to anarchist principles.

# Syndicalism

Syndicalism, also called anarcho-syndicalism, or revolutionary syndicalism, is a movement that advocates direct action by the working class to abolish the capitalist order, including the state, and to establish in its place a social order based on workers organized in production units. The syndicalist movement flourished in France chiefly between 1900 and 1914 and had a considerable impact in Spain, Italy, England, the Latin-American countries, and elsewhere. It had ceased to be a strong, dynamic force by the end of World War I, but it remained a residual force in Europe until World War II.

Syndicalism developed out of strong anarchist and antiparliamentary traditions among the French working class. Greatly influenced by the teachings of the anarchist Pierre-Joseph Proudhon and the socialist Auguste Blanqui, it was developed as a doctrine by certain leaders of the French trade-union movement toward the end of the 19th century. In France, syndicalism is known as *syndicalisme révolutionnaire* (the word *syndicalisme* means only "trade unionism"). Syndicalist tendencies manifested themselves with increasing strength during the 1890s in the two main French labour organizations of the period—the Confédération Générale du Travail (CGT) and the Fédération des Bourses du Travail. The secretary of the latter, Fernand Pelloutier, did much to work out the characteristic tenets of syndicalism and to spread them among his workers. When these two organizations joined forces in 1902, trade unionism, and syndicalism in particular, gained an immense accession of strength.

The syndicalist, like the Marxist, was opposed to capitalism and looked forward to an ultimate class war from which the working class would emerge victorious. To the syndicalist, the state was by nature a tool of capitalist oppression and, in any event, was inevitably rendered inefficient and despotic by its bureaucratic structure. As an appendage of the capitalist order, then, the state could not be used for reform with peaceful means and must be abolished.

The structure of the ideal syndicalist community was generally envisioned somewhat as follows. The unit of organization would be the local *syndicat*, a free association of self-governing "producers." It would be in touch with other groups through the local *bourse du travail* ("labour exchange"), which would function as a combination of employment and economic planning agency. When all the producers were thus linked together by the *bourse*, its administration—consisting of elected representatives of the members—would be able to estimate the capacities and necessities of the region, could coordinate production, and, being in touch through other *bourses* with the industrial system as a whole, could arrange for the necessary transfer of materials and commodities, inward and outward.

In keeping with their conception of the state as a tool of capitalist oppression, the syndicalists shunned political means of achieving their goals. This reliance upon direct industrial action stemmed from practical considerations as well: outside the mine or factory, the syndicalists realized, political differences among workers would come into play, possibly hindering mass action. Inside, their similar employment gave workers a sense of solidarity. Georges Sorel, a leading syndicalist theoretician, developed the concept of the "social myth," which could be used to stir workers to revolutionary action. The general strike, the preeminent syndicalist tool, was conceived of in these terms. If successful, it inspires workers with a sense of power; if unsuccessful, it impresses upon them the servility of their lot and the need for better organization and wider aims.

In the United States the Industrial Workers of the World embraced a form of syndicalism but aimed for a system based on large, centralized unions rather than on local associations. The Italian fascist dictatorship of Benito Mussolini sought to use syndicalist sentiment to gain support for its corporate state, which was in fact very much at variance with the syndicalist model in emphasizing a strong state.

After World War I, syndicalists tended to be lured away from the movement either by the Soviet model of communism or by the prospects for working-class gains offered by trade unionism and parliamentarianism in the Western republics. During the early years of Soviet power, in 1920–21, quasi-syndicalist ideas were prevalent among the trade-union communists' opposition movement, which acquired the name of "Workers' Opposition."

## Anarchism in Spain

The reconciliation of anarchism and syndicalism was most complete and most successful in Spain; for a long period the anarchist movement in that country remained the most numerous and the most powerful in the world. The first known Spanish anarchist, Ramón de la Sagra, a disciple of Proudhon, founded the world's first anarchist journal, *El Porvenir*, in La Coruña in 1845, which was quickly suppressed. Mutualist ideas were later publicized by Francisco Pi y Margall, a federalist leader and the translator of many of Proudhon's books. During the Spanish revolution of 1873, Pi y Margall attempted to establish a decentralized, or "cantonalist," political system on Proudhonian lines. In the end, however, the influence of Bakunin was stronger. In 1868 his Italian disciple, Giuseppe Fanelli, visited Barcelona and Madrid, where he established branches of the International. By 1870 they had 40,000 members, and in 1873 the movement numbered about 60,000, organized mainly in working men's associations. In 1874 the anarchist movement in

Spain was forced underground, a phenomenon that recurred often in subsequent decades. Nevertheless, it flourished, and anarchism became the favoured type of radicalism among two very different groups, the factory workers of Barcelona and other Catalan towns and the impoverished peasants who toiled on the estates of absentee owners in Andalusia.

As in France and Italy, the movement in Spain during the 1880s and '90s was inclined toward insurrection (in Andalusia) and terrorism (in Catalonia). It retained its strength in working-class organizations because the courageous and even ruthless anarchist militants were often the only leaders who would stand up to the army and to the employers, who hired squads of gunmen to engage in guerrilla warfare with the anarchists in the streets of Barcelona. The workers of Barcelona were finally inspired by the success of the French CGT to set up a syndicalist organization, Workers' Solidarity (Solidaridad Obrera), in 1907. Solidaridad Obrera quickly spread throughout Catalonia, and, in 1909, when the Spanish army tried to conscript Catalan reservists to fight against the Riffs in Morocco, it called a general strike. The work was followed by a week of largely spontaneous violence ("La Semana Tragica," or the Tragic Week) that left hundreds dead and 50 churches and monasteries destroyed and that ended in brutal repression. The torture of anarchists in the fortress of Montjuich and the execution of the internationally celebrated advocate of free education Francisco Ferrer led to worldwide protests and the resignation of the conservative government in Madrid. These events also resulted in a congress of Spanish trade unionists at Sevilla in 1910, which founded the National Confederation of Labour (Confederación Nacional del Trabajo; CNT).

The CNT, which included the majority of organized Spanish workers, was dominated throughout its existence by the anarchist militants, who in 1927 founded their own activist organization, the Iberian Anarchist Federation (Federación

Anarquista Iberica; FAI). While there was recurrent conflict within the CNT between moderates and FAI activists, the atmosphere of violence and urgency in which radical activities were carried on in Spain ensured that the more extreme leaders, such as Garcia Oliver and Buenaventura Durutti, tended to wield decisive influence. The CNT was a model of anarchist decentralism and antibureaucratism: its basic organizations were not national unions but *sindicatos únicos* ("special unions"), which brought together the workers of all trades and crafts in a certain locality; the national committee was elected each year from a different locality to ensure that no individual served more than one term; and all delegates were subject to immediate recall by the members. This enormous organization, which claimed 700,000 members in 1919, 1,600,000 in 1936, and more than 2,000,000 during the Civil War, employed only one paid secretary. Its day-to-day operation was carried on in their spare time by workers chosen by their comrades. This ensured that the Spanish anarchist movement would not be dominated by the déclassé intellectuals and self-taught printers and shoemakers who were so influential in other countries.

The CNT and the FAI, which remained clandestine organizations under the dictatorship of Miguel Primo de Rivera, emerged into the open with the abdication of King Alfonso XIII in 1931. Their antipolitical philosophy led them to reject the Republic as much as the monarchy it had replaced, and between 1931 and the military rebellion led by Francisco Franco in 1936 there were several unsuccessful anarchist risings. In 1936 the anarchists, who over the decades had become expert urban guerrillas, were mainly responsible for the defeat of the rebel generals in both Barcelona and Valencia, as well as in country areas of Catalonia and Aragon; and for many early months of the Civil War they were in virtual control of eastern Spain, where they regarded the crisis as an opportunity to carry through the social revolution of which they had long dreamed. Factories and railways in Catalonia were taken over by workers' committees, and in hundreds of villages in Catalonia, Levante, and Andalusia the peasants seized the land and established libertarian communes like those described by Kropotkin in *The Conquest of Bread*. The internal use of money was abolished, the land was tilled in common, and village products were sold or exchanged on behalf of the community in general, with each family receiving an equitable share of food and other necessities. An idealistic Spartan fervour characterized these communities, which often consisted of illiterate labourers; intoxicants, tobacco, and sometimes even coffee were renounced; and millenarian enthusiasm took the place of religion, as it has often done in Spain. The reports of critical observers suggest that at least some of these communes were efficiently run and more productive agriculturally than the villages had been previously.

The Spanish anarchists failed during the Civil War largely because, expert though they were in spontaneous street fighting, they did not have the discipline necessary to carry on sustained warfare; the columns they sent to various fronts were unsuccessful in comparison with the communist-led International Brigades. In December 1936 four leading anarchists took posts in the cabinet of Francisco Largo Caballero, radically compromising their antigovernment principles. They were unable to halt the trend toward left-wing totalitarianism encouraged by their enemies the communists, who were numerically far fewer but politically more influential, owing to the Soviet Union's support of the Republican war effort. In May 1937 bitter fighting broke out in Barcelona between communists and anarchists. The CNT held its own on this occasion, but its influence quickly waned. The collectivized factories were taken over by the central government, and many agricultural communes were destroyed by Franco's advance into Andalusia and by the hostile action of General Enrique Lister's communist army in Aragon. In January 1939 the Spanish anarchists were so demoralized by the compromises of the Civil War that they were unable to mount a resistance when Franco's forces marched into Barcelona. The CNT and the FAI became phantom organizations in exile.

# Decline of European Anarchism

By the time of the Spanish Civil War, the anarchist movement outside Spain had been destroyed or greatly diminished as a result of the Russian Revolution of 1917 and the rise of right-wing totalitarian regimes. Although the most famous anarchist leaders, Bakunin and Kropotkin, had been Russian, the anarchist movement had never been strong in Russia, partly because the larger Socialist Revolutionary Party had greater appeal to the peasantry. After the revolution the small anarchist groups that emerged in Petrograd (now St. Petersburg) and Moscow were powerless against the Bolsheviks. Kropotkin, who returned from exile in June 1917, found himself without influence, though he did establish an anarchist commune in the village of Dmitrov, near Moscow. A large demonstration of anarchists accompanied Kropotkin's funeral in 1921. In the south, N.I. Makhno, a peasant anarchist, raised an insurrectionary army that used brilliant guerrilla tactics to hold a large part of Ukraine from both the Red and the White armies; but the social experiments developed under Makhno's protection were rudimentary, and when he was driven into exile in 1921 the anarchist movement became extinct in Russia.

In other countries, the prestige of the Russian Revolution enabled the new communist parties to win much of the support formerly given to the anarchists, particularly in

*The storming of the Winter Palace in St. Petersburg, Russia, during the Russian Revolution, October 1917.* Universal Images Group/Getty Images

France, where the CGT passed permanently into communist control. The large Italian anarchist movement was destroyed by the fascist government of Benito Mussolini in the 1920s, and the small German anarchist movement was smashed by the Nazis in the 1930s.

# Anarchism in the Americas

In the United States, a native and mainly nonviolent tradition of anarchism developed during the 19th century in the writings of Henry David Thoreau, Josiah Warren, Lysander Spooner, Joseph Labadie, and, above all, Benjamin Tucker. An early advocate of women's suffrage, religious tolerance, and fair labour legislation, Tucker combined Warren's ideas on labour egalitarianism with elements of Proudhon's and Bakunin's antistatism. The result was the most sophisticated exposition to date of anarchist ideas in the United States. Much of Tucker's political influence, especially during the 1880s, derived from his journal *Liberty*, which he published in both Boston and New York City. Anarchist activism in the United States was mainly sustained by immigrants from Europe, including Johann Most (editor of *Die Freiheit*; "Freedom"), who justified acts of terrorism on anarchist principles; Alexander Berkman, who attempted to assassinate steel magnate Henry Clay Frick in 1892; and Emma Goldman, whose *Living My Life* gives a picture of radical activity in the United States at the turn of the century. Goldman, who had immigrated to the United States from tsarist Russia in 1885, soon became a preeminent figure in the American anarchist movement. A follower of Kropotkin, she lectured widely and published numerous essays on anarchist theory and practice in her journal *Mother Earth*. Most of her campaigns were controversial. She argued on behalf of birth control, defended the bomb throwers of her era as victims of a ruthless capitalist system, opposed women's suffrage—because, in her view, it would only further bind women to bourgeois reformism—and spoke out against American entry into World War I, which she believed was an imperialist war that was sacrificing ordinary people as cannon fodder.

Although anarchists were more often the victims of violence than its perpetrators, the cartoonists' stereotype of the long-haired, wild-eyed anarchist assassin emerged in the 1880s and was firmly established in the public mind during the Chicago Haymarket Riot of 1886.

The incident created widespread hysteria against immigrants and labour leaders and led to renewed suppression by police. Although the identity of the bomb thrower was never determined, eight anarchist leaders were arrested and charged with murder and conspiracy. Four members of the "Chicago Eight" were hanged on Nov. 11, 1887; one committed suicide in his cell; and three others were given long prison sentences. Excoriating the trial as unjust, Illinois Gov. John Peter Altgeld pardoned the three surviving Haymarket prisoners in 1893. May Day—International Workers' Day—was directly inspired by the Haymarket affair, and anarchists such as Goldman, Berkman, and Voltairine de Cleyre, as well as socialist Eugene V. Debs, traced their political awakenings to the events at Haymarket.

In 1901 an immigrant Polish anarchist, Leon Czolgosz, assassinated President McKinley. In 1903 Congress passed a law barring all foreign anarchists from entering or remaining in the country. In the repressive mood that followed World War I, anarchism in the United States was suppressed. Berkman, Goldman, and many other activists were imprisoned and deported. In a sensational trial in the spring of 1920, two immigrant Italian anarchists, Nicola Sacco and Bartolomeo Vanzetti, were convicted of killing a payroll clerk and a guard during a robbery at a Massachusetts shoe factory. In apparent retaliation for the conviction, a bomb was set off in the Wall

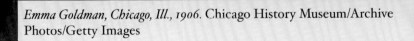

*Emma Goldman, Chicago, Ill., 1906.* Chicago History Museum/Archive Photos/Getty Images

Street area of New York City, killing more than 30 people and injuring 200 others. Despite worldwide protests that raised serious questions about the guilt of the defendants, Sacco and Vanzetti were executed in 1927.

In Latin America, strong anarchist elements were involved in the Mexican Revolution. The syndicalist teachings of Ricardo Flores Magon influenced the peasant revolutionism of Emiliano Zapata. After the deaths of Zapata in 1919 and Flores Magon in 1922, the revolutionary image in Mexico, as elsewhere, was taken over by communists. In Argentina and Uruguay there were significant anarcho-syndicalist movements early in the 20th century, but they too were greatly reduced by the end of the 1930s through intermittent repression and the competition of communism.

# Haymarket Riot

The Haymarket Riot, also called the Haymarket Affair or Haymarket Massacre, was a violent confrontation between police and labour protesters in Chicago on May 4, 1886, that became a symbol of the international struggle for workers' rights. It has been associated with May Day (May 1) since its designation as International Workers' Day by the Second International in 1889.

On May 3 one person was killed and several injured as police intervened to protect strikebreakers and intimidate strikers during a union action at the McCormick Harvesting Machine Company that was part of a national campaign to secure an eight-hour workday. To protest police brutality, anarchist labour leaders called a mass meeting the next day in Haymarket Square. That gathering was pronounced peaceful by Chicago Mayor Carter Harrison, who attended as an observer. After Harrison and most of the demonstrators

*Wood engraving of the Haymarket Riot by Thure de Thulstrup, published in* Harper's Weekly *on May 15, 1886.* Library of Congress, Washington, D.C.

departed, a contingent of police arrived and demanded that the crowd disperse. At that point a bomb was thrown by an individual never positively identified, and police responded with random gunfire. Seven police officers were killed and 60 others wounded before the violence ended; civilian casualties have been estimated at four to eight dead and 30 to 40 injured.

The Haymarket Riot created widespread hysteria directed against immigrants and labour leaders. Amid the panic, August Spies and seven other anarchists were convicted of murder on the grounds that they had conspired with or aided an unknown assailant. Many of the so-called "Chicago Eight," however, were not even present at the May 4 event, and their alleged involvement was never proved. Nevertheless, Spies and three other defendants were hanged on Nov. 11, 1887, while another defendant committed suicide.

In 1893 Illinois Gov. John Peter Altgeld was petitioned by the criminal attorney Clarence Darrow and others to grant clemency to the surviving three men. Studying the transcript

# Sacco-Vanzetti Case

The Sacco-Vanzetti case was a controversial murder trial in Massachusetts, U.S., extending over seven years, 1920–27, resulting in the execution of the defendants, Nicola Sacco and Bartolomeo Vanzetti.

The trial resulted from the murders in South Braintree, Mass., on April 15, 1920, of F.A. Parmenter, paymaster of a shoe factory, and Alessandro Berardelli, the guard accompanying him, in order to secure the payroll that they were carrying. On May 5 Sacco and Vanzetti, two Italian anarchists who had immigrated to the United States in 1908, one a shoemaker and the other a fish peddler, were arrested for the crime. On

*Bartolomeo Vanzetti* (center) *and Nicola Sacco* (right) *in handcuffs, circa 1920.* Fotosearch/Archive Photos/Getty Images

May 31, 1921, they were brought to trial before Judge Webster Thayer of the Massachusetts Superior Court, and on July 14 both were found guilty by verdict of the jury. Socialists and radicals protested the men's innocence. Many people felt that the trial had been less than fair and that the defendants had been convicted for their radical, anarchist beliefs rather than for the crime for which they had been tried. All attempts for retrial on the ground of false identification failed. On Nov. 18, 1925, Celestino Madeiros, then under a sentence for murder, confessed that he had participated in the crime with the Joe Morelli gang. The state supreme court refused to upset the verdict, because at that time the trial judge had the final power to reopen on the ground of additional evidence. The two men were sentenced to death on April 9, 1927.

A storm of protest arose with mass meetings throughout the nation. Massachusetts Gov. Alvan T. Fuller appointed an independent advisory committee consisting of President A. Lawrence Lowell of Harvard University, President Samuel W. Stratton of the Massachusetts Institute of Technology, and Robert Grant, a former judge. On Aug. 3, 1927, the governor refused to exercise his power of clemency; his advisory committee agreed with this stand. Demonstrations proceeded in many cities throughout the world, and bombs were set off in New York City and Philadelphia. Sacco and Vanzetti, still maintaining their innocence, were executed on Aug. 23, 1927.

Opinion has remained divided on whether Sacco and Vanzetti were guilty as charged or whether they were innocent victims of a prejudiced legal system and a mishandled trial. Some writers have claimed that Sacco was guilty but that Vanzetti was innocent. Many historians believe, however, that the two men should have been granted a second trial in view of their trial's significant defects.

On the 50th anniversary of their deaths in 1977, the governor of Massachusetts, Michael S. Dukakis, issued a proclamation stating that Sacco and Vanzetti had not been treated justly and that no stigma should be associated with their names.

of the case, Altgeld concluded that the defendants had not been given a fair trial because the judge was biased, the jury packed in the prosecution's favour, and much of the evidence fabricated. His decision to issue the pardons was widely condemned by industrialists and the conservative press but was applauded by labour reformers.

The Haymarket Riot had a lasting effect on the labour movement in the United States. The Knights of Labor (KOL), at the time the largest and most successful union organization in the country, was blamed for the incident. While the KOL also had sought an eight-hour day and had called several strikes to achieve that goal, its involvement in the riot could not be proved. Public distrust, however, caused many KOL locals to join the newly formed and less-radical American Federation of Labor.

The Haymarket tragedy inspired generations of labour leaders, leftist activists, and artists and has been commemorated in monuments, murals, and posters throughout the world, especially in Europe and Latin America. In 1893 the Haymarket Martyrs Monument was erected in a cemetery in the Chicago suburb of Forest Park. A statue dedicated to the slain police officers, erected in Haymarket Square in 1889, was moved to the Chicago Police Department's training academy in the early 1970s after it was repeatedly damaged by leftist radicals. An official commemoration, the Haymarket Memorial, was installed on the site of the riot in 2004.

# Anarchism in East Asia

During the first two decades of the 20th century, anarchism was by far the most significant current in radical thinking in East Asia. Although East Asian anarchists did not make significant original contributions to anarchist theory, they did introduce a number of important ideas to the politics and culture of their countries, including universal education, the rights of youth and women, and the need to abolish all divisions of labour—especially those between mental and manual labour and between agricultural and industrial labour. Perhaps the most significant and lasting of their contributions was the idea of "social revolution"—i.e., the idea that revolutionary political change cannot occur without radical changes in society and culture, specifically the elimination of social institutions that are inherently coercive and authoritarian, such as the traditional family. Although some anarchists in East Asia sought to create revolution through violence, others repudiated violence in favour of peaceful means, especially education. Nevertheless, they all believed that politics is determined mainly by society and culture and therefore that society and culture must be the focus of their revolutionary efforts.

## Anarchism in Japan

The first self-described anarchist in East Asia was the Japanese writer and activist Kōtoku Shūsui. In 1901 Kōtoku, an early advocate of Japanese socialism, helped to found the Social Democratic Party, which was immediately banned by the government. Early in 1905, after the newspaper he published, the *Heimin shimbun* ("Commoner's Newspaper"), denounced the Russo-Japanese War, the paper was closed and Kōtoku was imprisoned. While in prison he was profoundly influenced by anarchist literature—especially Kropotkin's *Fields, Factories, and Workshops*—and adopted anarchism wholeheartedly. As he wrote to a friend at the time, he had "gone [to prison] as a Marxian socialist and returned a radical anarchist." After five months in prison Kōtoku traveled to the United States, where he collaborated with

# Kōtoku Shūsui

Kōtoku Shūsui (Nov. 4, 1871–Jan. 24, 1911) was a socialist leader, one of the first proponents of radical political action in Japan. His execution resulted in the temporary abatement of the growing socialist movement in Japan.

Of relatively humble origin, Kōtoku started work as a houseboy in the Tokyo home of Hayashi Yūzō, one of the most famous liberal politicians of his day. He obtained an education and in 1893 became a newspaper writer. One of the earliest advocates of socialism in Japan, Kōtoku helped organize the Social Democratic Party in 1901. The party was immediately banned by the government, however, and Kōtoku, together with Sakai Toshihiko, then began his own newspaper, the *Heimin shimbun* ("Commoner's Newspaper"). After it opposed the Russo-Japanese War (1904–05), the paper was closed and Kōtoku was imprisoned. Released after five months, he toured the United States, where he was impressed by the direct action policies of a radical U.S. labour group, the "Wobblies" (Industrial Workers of the World).

Returning to Japan, he denounced parliamentary politics and began to organize workers for radical activities. This movement was crushed, however, when in 1910 hundreds were arrested on charges of being involved in a plot to assassinate the emperor. Although Kōtoku had withdrawn from the conspiracy, and at the end only four men were shown to be actually involved, Kōtoku was included among the 11 who were imprisoned and subsequently executed. The backlash resulting from the plot ended the socialist movement as a major force in Japan for almost a decade. Kōtoku spent the last months of his life writing articles denouncing Christianity.

members of the IWW, popularly known as the "Wobblies." His experiences in the United States led him to abandon parliamentary politics in favour of a violent strategy of "direct action."

After his return to Japan in June 1906, Kōtoku began organizing workers for radical activities. He also managed to persuade the newly founded Socialist Party of Japan to adopt his views on direct action. In 1910 Kōtoku was among hundreds arrested for involvement in a conspiracy to assassinate the Meiji emperor. Although he had withdrawn from the conspiracy before his arrest, Kōtoku was tried for treason and was executed in 1911. His death marked the beginning of a "winter period" for anarchism in Japan, which was to last until the end of World War I.

Although much diminished, anarchist activity in Japan did not completely cease during this period. Osugi Sakae, the foremost figure in Japanese anarchism in the decade after Kōtoku's death, published anarchist newspapers and led organizing campaigns among industrial workers. His efforts were hampered by continuous police repression, however, and he had very little impact in Japan. Nevertheless, Osugi greatly influenced anarchists in China and, later, Korea.

## Anarchism in China

Shortly after 1900, as part of the reforms that followed the unsuccessful Boxer Rebellion, the Ch'ing dynasty began to send many young Chinese to study abroad, especially in France, Japan, and the United States. In these places and elsewhere, Chinese students established nationalist and revolutionary organizations dedicated to overthrowing the imperial regime. Two of the most important of these groups—the World Association, founded in Paris in 1906, and the Society for the Study of Socialism, founded in Tokyo in 1907—adopted explicitly anarchist programs.

Between 1907 and 1910 the World Association published a journal, *The New Century*, that was a major source of information in Chinese on anarchist theory and the European anarchist movement. The journal promoted an individualistic and "futuristic" anarchism and was among the first Chinese-language publications to openly attack native traditions, in particular Confucianism. The Society for the Study of Socialism, on the other hand, favoured an antimodern anarchism influenced by the pacifist radicalism of Russian novelist Leo Tolstoy, and it stressed the affinity between anarchism and philosophical currents in the Chinese past, especially Taoism. Through its publications, *Natural Justice* and *Balance*, the Society advocated Kropotkin's programs for combining agriculture with industry and mental with manual labour, ideas that were to have a lasting influence on Chinese radicalism.

Significant anarchist activity in China itself did not begin until after the Chinese Revolution (1911–12). Chinese anarchists educated in Paris (the so-called "Paris anarchists") returned to Beijing and immediately became involved in the reform of education and culture. Convinced of the need for social revolution, the Paris anarchists argued in favour of Western science against religion and superstition, called for the emancipation of women and youth, rejected the traditional family and the Confucian values on which it was based, and organized experimental work-study communities as alternatives to traditional forms of family and working life. These ideas and practices were extremely influential in the New Culture movement of the late 1910s and early 1920s. Led by the generation of intellectuals sent to study abroad, the movement was critical of all aspects of traditional Chinese culture and ethics and called for sweeping reforms in existing political and social institutions.

Anarchists were also active in South China. In Canton, a native school of anarchism emerged around the charismatic revolutionary Liu Shifu, better known by his adopted name Shifu. In 1912 Shifu founded the Cock-Crow Society, whose journal, *People's Voice*, was the leading organ of Chinese anarchism in the 1910s. Although not a particularly original thinker, Shifu was a skilled expositor of anarchist doctrine. His polemical exchanges with the socialist leader Jiang Khangu helped to popularize anarchism as a "pure socialism" and to distinguish it from other currents in socialist thought.

## Anarchism in Vietnam and Korea

Anarchist ideas entered Vietnam through the activities of the early Vietnamese nationalist leader Phan Boi Chau. Chau, who led the struggle against French colonial rule during the first two decades of the 20th century, was introduced to anarchism by Chinese intellectuals in Tokyo in 1905–09. Although Chau was not an anarchist himself, his thinking reflected certain distinctly anarchist themes, notably anti-imperialism and "direct action." After the Chinese Revolution in 1911, Chau moved to South China, where he joined a number of organizations that espoused or were influenced by anarchism, including the Worldwide League for Humanity. He also received advice and financial support from Shifu. In 1912, with Shifu's help, he founded the League of the Restoration of Vietnam and the League for the Prosperity of China and Asia, which aimed to build links between revolutionary movements in China and those in colonized countries such as Vietnam, Burma (Myanmar), India, and Korea.

In the early 1920s Korean radicals established anarchist societies in Tokyo and in various locations in China. Like their counterparts in Vietnam, they were drawn to anarchism mostly for its anti-imperialism and its emphasis on direct action, which offered a justification for violent resistance to the Japanese colonial government. For leaders such as Shin Chaoe-ho, anarchism was an attractive democratic alternative to Bolshevik communism, which by this time was threatening to take control of the radical movement in Korea.

## Decline of Anarchism in East Asia

By the early 1920s anarchism in most parts of East Asia had entered a decline from which it would not recover. After the Russian Revolution of 1917, Bolshevik communists in Japan, China, Vietnam, and Korea established their own revolutionary societies, which were eventually transformed into clandestine political parties, and began to compete with anarchists for influence in the labour movements. Faced with the Bolsheviks' superior organizational abilities and the financial support they received from the newly constituted Soviet Union, the anarchists could offer only weak resistance and were soon eclipsed. By 1927, Chinese anarchists were devoting most of their energies to this losing struggle, sometimes in collusion with reactionary elements in the loosely structured Kuomintang (Nationalist Party). In Japan anarchist activity enjoyed a brief resurgence in the mid-1920s under Hatta Shuzo, who formulated a doctrine of "pure" anarchism in opposition to Marxist influences. A period of conflict between such pure and Marxist-oriented anarchists ended in the early 1930s, when all forms of radicalism were crushed by the military government.

## Phan Boi Chau

Phan Boi Chau (1867–Sept. 29, 1940) was a dominant personality of early Vietnamese resistance movements whose impassioned writings and tireless schemes for independence earned him the reverence of his people as one of Vietnam's greatest patriots.

Phan Boi Chau was the son of a poor scholar who stressed education and preparation for the mandarin examinations, the only means to success in the traditional bureaucracy. By the time he received his doctorate in 1900, Chau had become a firm nationalist.

In 1903 he wrote *Luu cau huyet le tan thu* ("Ryukyu's Bitter Tears"), an allegory equating Japan's bitterness at the loss of the Ryukyu Islands with the Vietnamese loss of independence. With fellow revolutionaries he formed the Duy Tan Hoi ("Reformation Society") in 1904 and secured the active support of Prince Cuong De, thus presenting to the people an alliance of royalty and resistance.

In 1905 Chau moved his resistance movement to Japan, and in 1906 he met the Chinese revolutionary Sun Yat-sen. His plans to place Cuong De on the throne of Vietnam resulted in a meeting in 1906 with the prince and the Vietnamese reformer Phan Chau Trinh. A Franco-Japanese understanding forced Chau, the Vietnamese students he had brought to Japan, and Cuong De to leave Japan in 1908–09. By 1912 Chau had reluctantly given up his monarchist scheme. He reorganized the resistance movement in Canton, China, under the name Viet Nam Quang Phuc Hoi ("Vietnam Restoration Society"). The organization launched a plan to assassinate the French governor-general of Indochina, but the plan failed. Chau was imprisoned in Canton from 1914 to 1917; during his confinement he wrote *Nguc trung thu* ("Prison Notes"), a short autobiography.

Upon his release, Chau studied Marxist doctrine and resumed his resistance to the French. In June 1925 he was seized and taken to Hanoi, but hundreds of Vietnamese protested against his arrest. The French pardoned him and offered him a civil service position that he refused.

Chau lived out his later years in quiet retirement at Hue, under French surveillance. He wrote a second autobiography, replete with directives for future revolutionaries, and several volumes of poetry. Among his notable works are *Viet Nam vong quoc su* (1906; "History of the Loss of Vietnam"), renowned as Vietnam's first revolutionary history book, and *Hau Tran dat su* ("Strange Story of the Latter Tran"), a historical novel with political implications.

Although politically irrelevant after the early 1920s, anarchists in China continued to work toward social revolution in education and culture. The author Ba Jin wrote novels and short stories on anarchist themes that were widely popular in China in the 1930s and '40s, and Ba was elected to important literary and cultural organizations after the communist victory in the Chinese Civil War (1945–49). In 1927, a group of Paris anarchists helped to establish a short-lived Labour University in Shanghai, which put into practice the anarchist belief in combining mental and manual labour. This belief lingered long after the anarchist movement itself was gone, influencing debates on economic policy in the communist government in the decades after 1949.

## Anarchism in the Arts

The central ideals of anarchism—freedom, equality, and mutual aid—have inspired writers and artists throughout history. When anarchism became an organized movement in the mid-19th century, its adherents hailed an impressive number of renowned literary and artistic figures as precursors and allies. In an influential essay, "Anarchism in Literature" (published posthumously in 1914), the American anarchist poet Voltairine de Cleyre identified anarchist sensibilities in writers and philosophers as diverse as François Rabelais, Jean-Jacques Rousseau, and Émile Zola in France; Ralph Waldo Emerson, Henry David Thoreau, and Walt Whitman in the United States; Friedrich Nietzsche in Germany; and Leo Tolstoy in Russia.

Many of the central figures of early 20th-century anarchism were passionately interested in the arts. Several of them wrote extensively on artistic themes, including Peter Kropotkin, Emma Goldman, Gustav Landauer, and Camillo Berneri. Most anarchist periodicals published

*Friedrich Nietzsche, circa 1890.* Hulton Archive/Getty Images

original poetry and art, and many of them made culture and the arts their primary focus. The most widely circulated English-language anarchist magazine of the 1960s, *Anarchy*, devoted entire issues to poetry, science fiction, blues, theatre, and film.

From the time of Proudhon through the 1950s, most anarchists favoured a propagandistic style of art that treated themes of social protest, and they generally avoided art that was self-consciously abstract, inward looking, fantastic, or nihilistic, as was much of Modernist art during this period. Nevertheless, many Modernist artists participated in anarchist groups or aided anarchist causes. Emma Goldman's *Mother Earth*, for example, published two political cartoons by the American painter and photographer Man Ray, though it did not publish any of his post-Cubist or Dadaist art.

## Poetry and Prose

Anarchist presses published an enormous quantity of verse—indeed, before 1960 they published more poetry than all other forms of creative writing put together. Among the finest poets of anarchism was Voltairine de Cleyre, whom Emma Goldman considered the "most gifted and brilliant anarchist woman America ever produced." Although the anarchist themes of de Cleyre's work were typical of her generation—tributes to revolutionary martyrs, hymns to anarchist anniversaries, and songs of workers rising against tyranny—her powerful imagery and passionate lyricism distinguished her from all her contemporaries. Other notable American poets of anarchy in the 1910s and 20s were Irish-born Lola Ridge; Japanese-born Sadakichi Hartmann, reputed to be the first writer of haiku in English; IWW organizer Covington Hall; and IWW songwriter and humorist T-Bone Slim (Matt Valentine Huhta), who was renowned for his anarchist aphorisms ("Wherever you find injustice, the proper form of politeness is attack").

Sicilian-American Surrealist poet Philip Lamantia belonged to an Italian-language anarchist group in San Francisco in the 1940s and later became a leading member of the Beat movement. Kenneth Rexroth, mentor to many Beats, identified himself as an anarchist from his involvement in the 1920s in Chicago's Dil Pickle Club, a popular forum for lectures and debates on revolutionary topics. Other anarchist-oriented Beat poets included Diane di Prima and Gary Snyder, whose manifesto "Buddhist Anarchism" (1961) proved to be one of that decade's most influential anarchist writings. The humorous *Abomunist Manifesto* (1959), by African American Beat poet Bob Kaufman, also had a markedly anarchist flavour. (According to Kaufman, "Abomunists vote against everyone by not voting for anyone.") Both the *Journal* and Kaufman's *Manifesto* were published by City Lights press, founded with the City Lights bookshop in San Francisco in the early 1950s by the poet and anarchist sympathizer Lawrence Ferlinghetti.

Major anarchist poets writing in other languages included Pietro Gori in Italian; Ernst Toller and the Scottish-born John Henry Mackay in German; the Jewish worker-poet David Edelstadt in Yiddish; and Laurent Tailhade in French. Poetic anarchy was also the hallmark of French Surrealist poets such as Benjamin Péret, who fought in an anarchist brigade in the Spanish Civil War.

Anarchism's creative writers also produced significant works of fiction. Under the influence of *Looking Backward, 2000–1887* (1888), the best-selling socialist utopian novel by the American writer Edward Bellamy, many anarchists de-vised utopias of their own—notably Lois Waisbrooker, whose *A Sex Revolution* (1892) blended anarchism and feminism, and J. William Lloyd, whose *The Natural Man: A Romance of* the *Golden Age* (1902) prefigured the counterculture of the 1960s. Largely owing to criticism by Kropotkin and other anarchists, Bellamy's *Equality* (1897), the sequel to *Looking Backward*, contained almost none of the earlier story's statist elements.

The mysterious German-language writer known as B. Traven, author of *The Cotton Pickers* (1926) and many other novels, may well be the most widely read anarchist storyteller of the 20th century. His tales excoriate statist intrusions upon individual existence, from passports and other bureaucratic paperwork to mass mobilization for war. *The Good Soldier Schweik* (1920–23), by the Czech author Jaroslav Hašek, is a hilarious satire of military life and bureaucracy and a classic of world literature, as is *The Family* (1931), by the Chinese anarchist Ba Jin.

Basic anarchist ideas, such as mistrust of state power, also have appeared in works by more mainstream American authors, such as Nelson Algren (who described himself as "basically against government"), Joseph Heller, Ursula Le Guin, and Edward Abbey, whose comic novel *The Monkey Wrench Gang* (1975) inspired Earth First!, the anarchist-oriented environmental movement.

## Ba Jin

Ba Jin (Nov. 25, 1904–Oct. 17, 2005) was a Chinese anarchist writer whose novels and short stories achieved widespread popularity in the 1930s and '40s.

Having been born to a wealthy gentry family, Li Yaotang received a traditional Confucian education as well as training in modern foreign languages and literatures. While in school, he developed socialist convictions and an interest in writing. He became an anarchist in the mid-1920s. After two years of study in France, he moved to Shanghai, where he wrote his first novel, *Miewang* ("Extinction"), which appeared with great success in 1929. He signed his work with the pen name Ba Jin, the last character of which is the Chinese equivalent of the last syllables of Peter Kropotkin, a Russian anarchist whom he admired.

During the next four years Ba Jin published seven novels, most of them dealing with social concerns and attacking the traditional family system. Most famous of these was the novel *Jia* (1933; "Family"). It was the first volume of the autobiographical trilogy *Jiliu* ("Torrent"), which was completed in 1940 with the publication of the second and third volumes, *Chun* ("Spring") and *Qiu* ("Autumn"). In the 1940s his writing became more pessimistic and less radical, and there was more truthful insight in his descriptions of human relationships; his most important novels of this period are *Qiyuan* (1944; "Pleasure Garden") and *Hanye* (1947; "Cold Nights").

Ba Jin's work was frequently attacked by the communists for both its content and its style, even though his numerous magazine articles and political activities on behalf of the left helped to create the emotional climate that allowed intellectuals to accept the communist revolution. After the establishment of the People's Republic of China in 1949, Ba Jin was judged politically reliable and was elected to important literary and cultural organizations. Although he formally renounced his anarchist ideas in the late 1950s, he never fully adapted himself to the new society, and he stopped writing fiction. During the Cultural Revolution (1966–76), he was labeled a counterrevolutionary and was sharply criticized. Ba Jin did not make a public appearance again until 1977, when he was rehabilitated. He was elected the vice chairman of the National Political Consultative Conference in 1983 and the chairman of the Chinese Writers Association in 1985.

Later translations of his works include *Living Amongst Heroes* (1954), *Autumn in Spring and Other Stories* (1981), and *Ward Four: A Novel of Wartime China* (1999).

## Theatre, Film, and Music

Emma Goldman's *The Social Significance of the Modern Drama* (1914) popularized the work of Henrik Ibsen and other European playwrights for American readers and helped to inspire the experimental little theatre movement in the United States. The Studio Players, an anarchist theatre company led by Lillian Udell, performed worker-oriented plays at the Radical Bookshop in Chicago throughout the 1920s. More avant-garde was The Living Theatre, founded in New York City in 1947 by Julian Beck and Judith Malina, which spearheaded a resurgence of anarchist theatre in the 1960s. Anarchist street theatre, replete with costumes, giant puppets, and dramatic stunts, became a mainstay of large protest demonstrations, such as those against the World Trade Organization (WTO) in Seattle in 1999.

An anarchist sensibility, characterized by ridicule of politicians, police, landlords, and other figures of authority, was evident early on in film in the work of Georges Méliès in France and in many American silent comedies of the 1910s and '20s, such as *Cops*, by Buster Keaton. More explicitly revolutionary were *The Golden Age* (1930), by the Surrealist Spanish filmmaker Luis Buñuel—which provoked a riot and was promptly banned—and works by the French director Jean Vigo, especially *Zero for Conduct* (1933). In the 1930s and '40s the film comedies of the French poet and screenwriter Jacques Prévert ridiculed all authoritarian values. In the 1950s and '60s the Greek filmmaker Adonis Kyrou, a collaborator on the Paris anarchist newspaper *Libertaire*, evoked the misery of war. Argentine-born Nelly Kaplan's *A Very Curious Girl* (1969)—which Pablo Picasso described as "insolence considered as one of the fine arts"—and *Néa* (1976) are classics of feminist anarchism.

Anarchists also made music. In the 1910s and '20s Rudolf von Liebich, music director of the Dil Pickle Club, composed songs and other music for the IWW. Avant-garde composer John Cage was an avowed anarchist. From the late 1970s many punk rock bands identified themselves with anarchy, and some—notably Crass and Chumbawumba in England and Fugazi in the United States—were actual anarchist collectives. Revolt and disrespect for authority were among their favourite themes. Anarchist critics and music historians also recognized a strong antiauthoritarian tradition in African American blues.

## Painting, Graphic Art, and Cartooning

Many major 20th-century painters, at one time or another, were active in the anarchist movement or acknowledged anarchism as a significant influence, including Pablo Picasso, Francis Picabia, and the Czech-born Marie Cermínová, known as Toyen, in France; Robert Henri, George Wesley Bellows, the Russian-born Max Weber, and Man Ray in the United States; Max Ernst in Germany; and Enrico Baj in Italy. Anarchist ideas affected all the major movements in painting—from the Ashcan School in the 1910s to Abstract Expressionism in the 1950s.

In the 1960s a new anarchist agitprop art began to flourish, largely inspired by Expressionism, Surrealism, and the work of the Mexican printmaker José Guadalupe Posada. The Italian painter Flavio Costantini's dramatic portrayals of anarchist history and the graphic art of Carlos Cortez, Eric Drooker, and Josh MacPhee in the United States and Clifford Harper in England were widely reproduced in anarchist magazines and as posters. Also striking are the imaginative collages of American artists Freddie Baer and James Koehnline.

Cartoons, always major weapons in the anarchist arsenal, were more prominent than ever in the movement's press at

Ubu Imperator *by Max Ernst, published in* La Révolution surréaliste.
Raphael Gaillarde/Gamma-Rapho/Getty Images

the end of the 20th century. Satirical sketches by Roberto Ambrosoli in Italy and Tuli Kupferberg in the United States appeared throughout the world. England's Freedom Press attracted many comic-strip artists, including Philip Sansom and German-born John Olday in the 1940s and later, from the 1960s through the 1990s, Arthur Moyse. Donald Rooum's inventive series *Wildcat* was collected in several volumes.

# Contemporary Anarchism

After World War II, anarchist groups and federations reemerged in almost all countries where they had formerly flourished—the notable exceptions being Spain and the Soviet Union—but these organizations wielded little influence compared to that of the broader movement inspired by earlier ideas. This development is not surprising, since anarchists never stressed the need for organizational continuity, and the cluster of social and moral ideas that are identifiable as anarchism always spread beyond any clearly definable movement.

Anarchist ideas emerged in a wider frame of reference beginning with the American civil rights movement of the 1950s, which aimed to resist injustice through the tactic of civil disobedience. In the 1960s and '70s a new radicalism took root among students and the left in general in the United States, Europe, and Japan, embracing a general criticism of "elitist" power structures and the materialist values of modern industrial societies—both capitalist and communist. For these radicals, who rejected the traditional parties of the left as strongly as they did the existing political structure, the appeal of anarchism was strong. The general anarchist outlook—with its emphasis on spontaneity, theoretical flexibility, simplicity of life, and the importance of love and anger as complementary and necessary components in both social and individual action—attracted those who opposed impersonal political institutions and the calculations of older parties. The anarchist rejection of the state, and the insistence on decentralism and local autonomy, found strong echoes among those who advocated participatory democracy. The anarchist insistence on direct action was reflected in calls for extraparliamentary action and violent confrontation by some student groups in France, the United States, and Japan. And the recurrence of the theme of workers' control of industry in so many manifestos of the 1960s—especially during the student uprisings in Paris in May 1968—showed the enduring relevance of anarcho-syndicalist ideas.

Beginning in the 1970s, anarchism became a significant factor in the radical ecology movement in the United States and Europe. Anarchist ideas in works by the American novelist Edward Abbey, for example, inspired a generation of eco-anarchists in the United States, including the radical Earth First! organization, to protest urban sprawl and the destruction of old-growth forests. Much influential work in anarchist theory during this period and afterward, such as that of Murray Bookchin, was noteworthy for its argument that statism and capitalism were incompatible with environmental preservation.

Anarchists also took up issues related to feminism and developed a rich body of work, known as anarcha-feminism, that applied anarchist principles to the analysis of women's oppression, arguing that the state is inherently patriarchal and that women's experience as nurturers and care-givers reflects the anarchist ideals of mutuality and the rejection of hierarchy and authority.

The most prevalent current in anarchist thinking during the last two decades of the 20th century (at least in the United States) was an eclectic, countercultural mixture of theories reflecting a wide range of artistic, literary, political, and philosophical influences, including Dada, Surrealism, and

Situationism; the writers of the Beat movement; the Frankfurt School of Marxist-oriented social and political philosophers—especially Herbert Marcuse—and post-structuralist and postmodern philosophy and literary theory, in particular the work of the French philosopher and historian Michel Foucault. Other influential figures were the American linguist and political writer Noam Chomsky, the Czech-born American writer and activist Fredy Perlman, and Hakim Bey and other writers associated with the anarchist publisher Autonomedia in New York City. African American anarchism, as represented in the writings of former Black Panther Lorenzo Kom'boa Ervin in the late 1970s, was a major influence in the United States and in many other parts of the world.

Although some older varieties of anarchism, such as Proudhonian Mutualism, had faded away by the end of the 20th century, others persisted, including the anarchist individualism of Warren, Spooner, and others in the United States and anarchist communism in Europe and Latin America. Anarcho-syndicalism remained a significant movement in Spain, France, Sweden, and parts of Africa and Latin America. As in the 1960s, anarchism continued to exert a strong appeal among students and young people, and a large percentage of those who considered themselves anarchists were in their teens and twenties. From the early 1970s the anarchist emblem consisting of a circled A was an established part of the iconography of global youth culture.

In 1999 anarchist-led demonstrations against the WTO in Seattle provoked wide media attention, as did later related protests against the World Bank and the International Monetary Fund (IMF). The unprecedented publicity given to the anarchists' explicitly revolutionary viewpoint inspired a proliferation of new anarchist groups, periodicals, and Internet sites. Anarchists were also a significant—and in some cases a predominating—influence in many other political movements, including campaigns against police brutality and capital punishment, the gay rights movement, and diverse movements promoting animal rights, vegetarianism, abortion rights, the abolition of prisons, the legalization of marijuana, and the abolition of automobiles.

At the beginning of the 21st century, no anarchist movement posed a serious threat to state power, and anarchists were no closer to achieving their dream of a society without government than they were a century before. Nevertheless, the perceived failure of governments to solve enduring social problems such as racial and gender inequality, poverty, environmental destruction, political corruption, and war increased the appeal of anarchist ideas among many groups. Young people in particular were attracted to the anarchist priorities of creativity and spontaneity—the importance of living the "new society" here and now rather than postponing it indefinitely until "after the Revolution." For these people and many others around the world, anarchism remained an active and vibrant ferment of criticism, protest, and direct action.

# CHAPTER 2

# REVOLUTION

Revolution in social and political science is a major, sudden, and hence typically violent alteration in government and in related associations and structures. The term is used by analogy in such expressions as the Industrial Revolution, where it refers to a radical and profound change in economic relationships and technological conditions.

Though the idea of revolution was originally related to the Aristotelian notion of cyclical alterations in the forms of government, it now implies a fundamental departure from any previous historical pattern. A revolution constitutes a challenge to the established political order and the eventual establishment of a new order radically different from the preceding one. The great revolutions of European history, especially the English, French, and Russian revolutions, changed not only the system of government but also the economic system, the social structure, and the cultural values of those societies.

Historically, the concept of revolution was seen as a very destructive force, from ancient Greece right through to the European Middle Ages. The ancient Greeks saw revolution as a possibility only after the decay of the fundamental moral and religious tenets of society. Plato believed that a constant, firmly entrenched code of beliefs could prevent revolution. Aristotle elaborated on this concept, concluding that if a culture's basic

*Outraged Ukrainians gather in Independence Square in Kiev on Dec. 1, 2013, to protest authorities rejecting a historic EU pact.* Sergei Supinsky/AFP/ Getty Images

value system is tenuous, the society will be vulnerable to revolution. Any radical alteration in basic values or beliefs provides the grounds for a revolutionary upheaval.

During the Middle Ages, the maintenance of the established beliefs and forms of government remained the priority. Much attention was given to finding means of combating revolution and stifling changes in society. Religious authority was so strong and its belief in the maintenance of order so fundamental that the church directed people to accept the inequities of power, instead of upsetting the stability of society.

Only after the emergence of secular humanism during the Renaissance did this concept of revolution, as a cause of the desecration of society, change to embrace a more modern perspective. The 16th-century Italian writer Niccolò

Machiavelli recognized the importance of creating a state that could endure the threat of revolution; but, at the same time, his detailed analysis of power led to a new belief in the necessity of changes in the structure of government on certain occasions. This new acceptance of change placed Machiavelli at the forefront of modern revolutionary thought, even though he never used the word "revolution" in his texts, and he was primarily concerned with the creation of a truly stable state.

The 17th-century English writer John Milton was an early believer in revolution's inherent ability to help a society realize its potential. He also saw revolution as the right of society to defend itself against abusive tyrants, creating a new order that reflected the needs of the people. To Milton, revolution was the means of accomplishing freedom. Later, in the 18th century, the French and American revolutions were attempts to secure freedom from oppressive leadership. Modern revolutions have frequently incorporated utopian ideals as a basis for change.

Immanuel Kant, an 18th-century German philosopher, believed in revolution as a force for the advancement of mankind. Kant believed that revolution was a "natural" step in the realization of a higher ethical foundation for society. This idea helped serve as a basis for the American and French revolutions.

The 19th-century German philosopher G.W.F. Hegel was a crucial catalyst in the formation of 20th-century revolutionary thought. He saw revolutions as the fulfillment of human destiny, and he saw revolutionary leaders as those necessary to instigate and implement reforms. Hegel's theories served as the foundation for the most influential revolutionary thinker, Karl Marx. Marx used Hegel's abstractions as the basis for a plan of class struggle, centred on a fight for the control of the economic processes of society. Marx believed in progressive stages of human history, culminating in the working-class overthrow of the property-owning class. For society to advance, the working class, or proletariat, must take over the means of production. Marx viewed this eventuality as the conclusion of the human struggle for freedom and a classless society, thus eliminating the need for further political change. Communist revolutions led by Marxists took place in Russia, Yugoslavia, China, Vietnam, and Cuba, among other countries, in the 20th century.

One modern historian, Crane Brinton, analyzed the tendencies of a society prior to a major revolution. He saw a pre-revolutionary society as having a combination of social and political tensions, caused by a gradual breakdown of the values of a society. This leads to a fracture of political authority, as the governing body must rely upon an increasingly desperate use of force to remain in power. Commensurate with this is the emergence of reform elements that serve to emphasize the corruption of the political authority. As the existing political order begins to lose its grasp on authority, momentum builds among the diverse forces of the opposition. As the government becomes more precarious, the splinter groups that form the threat to the existing order band together to topple the authority.

Brinton also observed the different stages of a major revolution. After the government is overthrown, there is usually a period of optimistic idealism, and the revolutionaries engage in much perfectionist rhetoric. But this phase does not last very long. The practical tasks of governing have to be faced, and a split develops between moderates and radicals. It ends in the defeat of the moderates, the rise of extremists, and the concentration of all power in their hands. For one faction to prevail and maintain its authority, the use of force is almost inevitable. The goals of the revolution fade as a totalitarian regime takes command. Some of the basic tenets of the original revolutionary movement, however, are eventually incorporated in the end. The French and Russian revolutions followed this course of development, as did the Islamic Revolution in Iran in the late 20th century.

A strictly political revolution, independent of social transformation, does not possess the same pattern of prerevolutionary and postrevolutionary events. It may be merely a change in political authority (as in many coups d'état) or a somewhat broader transformation of the structures of power (as in the American and Mexican revolutions).

# Iranian Revolution of 1978–79

Also called the Islamic Revolution (Persian Enqelāb-e Eslāmī), the Iranian Revolution was a popular uprising in Iran in 1978–79 that resulted in the toppling of the monarchy on April 1, 1979, and led to the establishment of an Islamic republic.

## Prelude to Revolution

Mounting social discontent in the 1970s in Iran, which culminated in revolution at the end of the decade, had several crucial dimensions. Although petroleum revenues continued to be a major source of income for Iran in the 1970s, world monetary instability and fluctuations in Western oil consumption seriously threatened the country's economy, which had been rapidly expanding since the early 1950s and was still directed in large part toward high-cost projects and programs. A decade of extraordinary economic growth, heavy government spending, and a boom in oil prices led to high rates of inflation and the stagnation of Iranians' buying power and standard of living.

In addition to mounting economic difficulties, sociopolitical repression by the regime of Mohammad Reza Shah Pahlavi likewise increased in the 1970s. Outlets for political participation were minimal, and opposition parties such as the National Front (a loose coalition of nationalists, clerics, and noncommunist left-wing parties) and the pro-Soviet Tūdeh ("Masses") Party were marginalized or outlawed. Social and political protest was often met with censorship, surveillance, or harassment, and illegal detention and torture were common.

Many argued that since Iran's brief experiment with parliamentary democracy and communist politics had failed, the country had to go back to its indigenous culture. The 1953 coup, backed by the U.S. Central Intelligence Agency (CIA), against Prime Minister Mohammad Mosaddeq, an outspoken advocate of nationalism who almost succeeded in deposing the shah, particularly incensed Iran's intellectuals. For the first time in more than half a century, the secular intellectuals—many of whom were fascinated by the populist appeal of Ayatollah Ruhollah Khomeini, a former professor of philosophy in Qom who had been exiled in 1964 after speaking out harshly against the shah's recent reform program—abandoned their aim of reducing the authority and power of the Shī'ite ulama (religious scholars) and argued that, with the help of the ulama, the shah could be overthrown.

In this environment, members of the National Front, the Tūdeh Party, and their various splinter groups now joined the ulama in a broad opposition to the shah's regime. Khomeini continued to preach in exile about the evils of the Pahlavi regime, accusing the shah of irreligion and subservience to foreign powers. Thousands of tapes and print copies of Khomeini's speeches were smuggled back into Iran during the 1970s as an increasing number of unemployed and working-poor Iranians—mostly new immigrants from the countryside, who were disenchanted by the cultural vacuum of modern urban Iran—turned to the ulama for guidance. The shah's dependence on the United States, his close ties

*Ayatollah Ruhollah Khomeini on Jan. 24, 1984, in Iran.* Francois Lochon/
Gamma-Rapho/Getty Images

with Israel—then engaged in extended hostilities with the overwhelmingly Muslim Arab states—and his regime's ill-considered economic policies served to fuel the potency of dissident rhetoric with the masses.

Outwardly, with a swiftly expanding economy and a rapidly modernizing infrastructure, everything was going well in Iran. But in little more than a generation, Iran had changed from a traditional, conservative, and rural society to one that was industrial, modern, and urban. The sense that in both agriculture and industry too much had been attempted too soon and that the government, either through corruption or incompetence, had failed to deliver all that was promised was manifested in demonstrations against the regime in 1978.

## Revolution

In January 1978, incensed by what they considered to be slanderous remarks made against Khomeini in *Eṭṭelāʿāt,* a Tehrān newspaper, thousands of young madrassa (religious school) students took to the streets. They were followed by thousands more Iranian youth—mostly unemployed recent immigrants from the countryside—who began protesting the regime's excesses. The shah, weakened by cancer and stunned by the sudden outpouring of hostility against him, vacillated between concession and repression, assuming the protests to be part of an international conspiracy against him. Many people were killed by government forces in anti-regime protests, serving only to fuel the violence in a Shīʿite country where martyrdom played a fundamental role in religious expression. Fatalities were followed by demonstrations to commemorate the customary 40-day milestone of mourning in Shīʿite tradition, and further casualties occurred at those protests, mortality and protest propelling one another forward. Thus, in spite of all government efforts, a cycle of violence began in which each death fueled further protest, and all protest—from the secular left and religious right—was subsumed under the cloak of Shī'ite Islam and crowned by the revolutionary rallying cry "Allāhu akbar" ("God is great"), which could be heard at protests and which issued from the rooftops in the evenings.

During his exile, Khomeini coordinated this upsurge of opposition—first from Iraq and after 1978 from France—demanding the shah's abdication. In January 1979, in what was officially described as a "vacation," the shah and his family fled Iran. The Regency Council established to run the country during the shah's absence proved unable to function, and Prime Minister Shahpur Bakhtiar, hastily appointed by the shah before his departure, was incapable of effecting compromise with either his former National Front colleagues or Khomeini. Crowds in excess of one million demonstrated in Tehrān, proving the wide appeal of Khomeini, who arrived in Iran amid wild rejoicing on February 1. Ten days later Bakhtiar went into hiding, eventually to find exile in France.

## Aftermath

On April 1, following overwhelming support in a national referendum, Khomeini declared Iran an Islamic republic. Elements within the clergy promptly moved to exclude their former left-wing, nationalist, and intellectual allies from any positions of power in the new regime, and a return to conservative social values was enforced. The Family Protection Act (1967; significantly amended in 1975), which provided further guarantees and rights to women in marriage, was declared void, and mosque-based revolutionary bands known as *komītehs* (Persian: "committees") patrolled the streets enforcing Islamic codes of dress and behaviour and dispatching impromptu justice to perceived enemies of the revolution. Throughout most of 1979 the Revolutionary Guards—then an informal religious militia formed by Khomeini to forestall another CIA-backed coup as in the days of Mosaddeq—engaged in similar activity, aimed at intimidating and repressing political groups not under control of the ruling Revolutionary Council and its sister Islamic Republican Party, both clerical organizations loyal to Khomeini. The violence and brutality often exceeded that which had taken place under the shah.

The militias and the clerics they supported made every effort to suppress Western cultural influence, and, facing persecution and violence, many of the Western-educated elite fled the country. This anti-Western sentiment eventually manifested itself in the November 1979 seizure of 66 hostages at the U.S. embassy by a group of Iranian protesters demanding the extradition of the shah, who at that time was undergoing medical treatment in the United States. Through the embassy takeover, Khomeini's supporters could claim to be as "anti-imperialist" as the political left. This ultimately gave them the ability to suppress most of the regime's left-wing and moderate opponents. The Assembly of Experts (Majles-e Khobregān), overwhelmingly dominated by clergy, ratified a new constitution the following month. The new constitution created a religious government based on Khomeini's vision of *velāyat-e faqīh* (Persian: "governance of the jurist") and gave sweeping powers to the *rahbar*, or leader; the first *rahbar* was Khomeini himself. Moderates, such as provisional Prime Minister Mehdi Bazargan and the republic's first president, Abolhasan Bani-Sadr, who opposed holding the hostages, were steadily forced from power by conservatives within the government who questioned their revolutionary zeal.

## Chinese Revolution

The Chinese Revolution (1911–12) was a nationalist democratic revolt that overthrew the Qing (or Manchu) dynasty in 1912 and created a republic. Ever since their conquest of China in the 17th century, most of the Manchu had lived in comparative idleness, supposedly a standing army of occupation but in reality inefficient pensionaries. All through the 19th century the dynasty had been declining, and, upon the death of the empress dowager Cixi (1908), it lost its last able leader. In 1911 the emperor Puyi was a child, and the regency was incompetent to guide the nation. The unsuccessful contests with foreign powers had shaken not only the dynasty but the entire machinery of government.

The chain of events immediately leading to the revolution began when an agreement was signed (April 5, 1911) with a four-power group of foreign bankers for the construction of lines on the Hukwang (Huguang) Railway in central China. The Beijing government decided to take over from a local company a line in Sichuan, on which construction had been barely begun, and to apply part of the loan to its completion. The sum offered did not meet the demands of the stockholders, and in September 1911 the dissatisfaction boiled over into open revolt. On October 10, in consequence of the uncovering of a plot in Hankou (now [along with Wuchang] part of Wuhan) that had little or no connection with the Sichuan episode, a mutiny broke out among the troops in Wuchang, and this is regarded as the formal beginning of the revolution. The mutineers soon captured the Wuchang mint and arsenal, and city after city declared against the Qing government. The regent, panic-stricken, granted the assembly's demand for the immediate adoption of a constitution and urged a former viceroy, Yuan Shikai, to come out of retirement and save the dynasty. In November he was made premier.

Had Yuan acted vigorously, he might have suppressed the uprising and so have delayed the inevitable. He dallied, however, and, by the end of the year, 14 provinces had declared against the Qing leadership. In several cities Manchu garrisons had been massacred, the regent had been forced out of office, a provisional republican government had been set up at Nanjing, and the archrevolutionist Sun Yat-sen (Sun Zhongshan) had returned from abroad and had been elected provisional president.

In December Yuan agreed to an armistice and entered upon negotiations with the republicans. On Feb. 12, 1912, the boy emperor was made to abdicate the throne in a proclamation that transferred the government to the people's representatives, declared that the constitution should thenceforth be republican, and gave Yuan Shikai full powers to organize a provisional government. The Nanjing authorities agreed that the emperor was to retain his title for life and receive a large pension. To unify the country, Sun Yat-sen resigned the presidency, and Yuan was chosen in his place. Li Yuanhong, who had come into prominence in Wuchang in the initial stages of the rebellion, was elected vice president. A provisional constitution was promulgated in March 1912 by the Nanjing parliament, and in April the government was transferred to Beijing.

The republic, established with such startling rapidity and comparative ease, was destined in the succeeding decades to witness the progressive collapse of national unity and orderly government.

## Taiping Rebellion

The Taiping Rebellion (1850–64) was a radical political and religious upheaval that was probably the most important event in China in the 19th century. It ravaged 17 provinces, took an estimated 20,000,000 lives, and irrevocably altered the Qing dynasty (1644–1911/12).

The rebellion began under the leadership of Hong Xiuquan (1814–64), a disappointed civil service examination candidate who, influenced by Christian teachings, had a series of visions and believed himself to be the son of God, the younger brother of Jesus Christ, sent to reform China. A friend of Hong's, Feng Yunshan, utilized Hong's ideas to organize a new religious group, the God Worshippers' Society (Bai Shangdi Hui), which he formed among the impoverished peasants of Guangxi province. In 1847 Hong joined Feng and the God Worshippers, and three years later he led them in rebellion. On Jan. 1, 1851, he proclaimed his new dynasty, the Taiping Tianguo ("Heavenly Kingdom of Great Peace"), and assumed the title of Tianwang, or "Heavenly King."

Their credo—to share property in common—attracted many famine-stricken peasants, workers, and miners, as did their propaganda against the foreign Manchu rulers of China. Taiping ranks swelled, and they increased from a ragged band of several thousand to more than 1,000,000 totally disciplined and fanatically zealous soldiers, organized into separate men's and women's divisions. Sweeping north through the fertile Yangtze River Valley, they reached the great eastern China city of Nanjing. After capturing the city on March 10, 1853, the Taipings halted. They renamed the city Tianjing ("Heavenly Capital") and dispatched a northern expedition to capture the Qing capital at Beijing. This failed, but another expedition into the upper Yangtze River (Chang Jiang) valley scored many victories.

Meanwhile, Yang Xiuqing, the Taiping minister of state, attempted to usurp much of the Tianwang's power, and as a result Yang and thousands of his followers were slain. Wei Changhui, the general who had slain Yang, then began to grow haughty, and Hong had him murdered as well. Another Taiping general, Shi Dakai, began to fear for his life, and he abandoned Hong, taking with him many of the Taiping followers.

*Painting of the Taiping Rebellion, circa 1850.* The Art Archive/SuperStock

In 1860 an attempt by the Taipings to regain their strength by taking Shanghai was stopped by the Western-trained "Ever-Victorious Army" commanded by the American adventurer Frederick Townsend Ward and later by the British officer Charles George ("Chinese") Gordon. The gentry, who usually rallied to support a successful rebellion, had been alienated by the radical anti-Confucianism of the Taipings, and they organized under the leadership of Zeng Guofan, a Chinese official of the Qing government. By 1862 Zeng had managed to surround Nanjing, and the city fell in July 1864. Hong, ailing and refusing all requests to flee the city, had committed suicide in June, though before that he had installed his 15-year-old son as the Tianwang. Sporadic Taiping resistance continued in other parts of the country until 1868.

Taiping Christianity placed little emphasis on New Testament ideas of kindness, forgiveness, and redemption. Rather it emphasized the wrathful Old Testament God who demanded worship and obedience. Prostitution, foot-binding, and slavery were prohibited, as well as opium smoking, adultery, gambling, and use of tobacco and alcohol. Organization of the army was elaborate, with strict rules governing soldiers in camp and on the march. For those who followed these rules, an ultimate reward was promised. Zeng Guofan was astonished when, after the capture of Nanjing, almost 100,000 of the Taiping followers preferred death to capture.

Under the Taipings, the Chinese language was simplified, and equality between men and women was decreed. All property was to be held in common, and equal distribution of the land according to a primitive form of communism was planned. Some Western-educated Taiping leaders even proposed the development of industry and the building of a Taiping democracy. The Qing dynasty was so weakened by the rebellion that it never again was able to establish an effective hold over the country. Both the Chinese communists and the Chinese Nationalists trace their origin to the Taipings.

## Russian Revolution of 1917

The Russian Revolution of 1917 was two revolutions, the first of which, in February (March, New Style), overthrew the imperial government and the second of which, in October (November), placed the Bolsheviks in power.

By 1917 the bond between the tsar and most of the Russian people had been broken. Governmental corruption and inefficiency were rampant. The tsar's reactionary policies, including the occasional dissolution of the Duma, or Russian parliament, the chief fruit of the 1905 revolution, had spread dissatisfaction even to moderate elements. The

Russian Empire's many ethnic minorities grew increasingly restive under Russian domination.

But it was the government's inefficient prosecution of World War I that finally provided the challenge the old regime could not meet. Ill-equipped and poorly led, Russian armies suffered catastrophic losses in campaign after campaign against German armies. The war made revolution inevitable in two ways: it showed Russia was no longer a military match for the nations of central and western Europe, and it hopelessly disrupted the economy.

Riots over the scarcity of food broke out in the capital, Petrograd (formerly St. Petersburg), on February 24 (March 8), and, when most of the Petrograd garrison joined the revolt, Tsar Nicholas II was forced to abdicate March 2 (March 15). When his brother, Grand Duke Michael, refused the throne, more than 300 years of rule by the Romanov dynasty came to an end.

A committee of the Duma appointed a Provisional Government to succeed the autocracy, but it faced a rival in the Petrograd Soviet of Workers' and Soldiers' Deputies. The 2,500 delegates to this soviet were chosen from factories and military units in and around Petrograd.

The Soviet soon proved that it had greater authority than the Provisional Government, which sought to continue Russia's participation in the European war. On March 1 (March 14) the Soviet issued its famous Order No. 1, which directed the military to obey only the orders of the Soviet and not those of the Provisional Government. The Provisional Government was unable to countermand the order. All that now prevented the Petrograd Soviet from openly declaring itself the real government of Russia was fear of provoking a conservative coup.

Between March and October the Provisional Government was reorganized four times. The first government was composed entirely of liberal ministers, with the exception of the Socialist Revolutionary Aleksandr F. Kerensky. The subsequent governments were coalitions. None of them, however, was able to cope adequately with the major problems afflicting the country: peasant land seizures, nationalist independence movements in non-Russian areas, and the collapse of army morale at the front.

Meanwhile, soviets on the Petrograd model, in far closer contact with the sentiments of the people than the Provisional Government was, had been organized in cities and major towns and in the army. In these soviets, "defeatist" sentiment, favouring Russian withdrawal from the war on almost any terms, was growing. One reason was that radical socialists increasingly dominated the soviet movement. At the First All-Russian Congress of Soviets, convened on June 3

*Vladimir Lenin speaking in Sverdlov Square, Moscow, May 5, 1920.* Universa Images Group/Getty Images

(June 16), the Socialist Revolutionaries were the largest single bloc, followed by the Mensheviks and Bolshcviks.

Kerensky became head of the Provisional Government in July and put down a coup attempted by army commander in chief Lavr Georgiyevich Kornilov (according to some historians, Kerensky may have initially plotted with Kornilov in the hope of gaining control over the Petrograd Soviet). However, he was increasingly unable to halt Russia's slide into political, economic, and military chaos, and his party suffered a major split as the left wing broke from the Socialist Revolutionary Party. But while the Provisional Government's power waned, that of the soviets was increasing, as was the Bolsheviks' influence within them. By September the Bolsheviks and their allies, the Left Socialist Revolutionaries, had overtaken the Socialist Revolutionaries and Mensheviks and held majorities in both the Petrograd and Moscow soviets.

By autumn the Bolshevik program of "peace, land, and bread" had won the party considerable support among the hungry urban workers and the soldiers, who were already deserting from the ranks in large numbers. Although a previous coup attempt (the July Days) had failed, the time now seemed ripe. On October 24–25 (November 6–7) the Bolsheviks and Left Socialist Revolutionaries staged a nearly bloodless coup, occupying government buildings, telegraph stations, and other strategic points. Kerensky's attempt to organize resistance proved futile, and he fled the country. The Second All-Russian Congress of Soviets, which convened in Petrograd simultaneously with the coup, approved the formation of a new government composed mainly of Bolshevik commissars.

## Glorious Revolution

The Glorious Revolution, also called the Revolution of 1688, or the Bloodless Revolution in English history, was the events of 1688–89 that resulted in the deposition of James II and the accession of his daughter Mary II and her husband, William III, prince of Orange and *stadholder* of the Netherlands.

After the accession of James II in 1685, his overt Roman Catholicism alienated the majority of the population. In 1687 he issued a Declaration of Indulgence, suspending the penal laws against dissenters and recusants, and in April 1688 ordered that a second Declaration of Indulgence be read from every pulpit on two successive Sundays. William Sancroft, the archbishop of Canterbury, and six other bishops petitioned him against this and were prosecuted for seditious libel. Their acquittal almost coincided with the birth of a son to James's Roman Catholic queen, Mary of Modena (June). This event promised an indefinite continuance of his policy and brought discontent to a head. Seven eminent Englishmen, including one bishop and six prominent politicians of both Whig and Tory persuasions, wrote inviting William of Orange to come over with an army to redress the nation's grievances.

William was both James's nephew and his son-in-law, and, until the birth of James's son, his wife, Mary, was heir apparent. William's chief concern was to check the overgrowth of French power in Europe, and he welcomed England's aid. Thus, having been in close touch with the leading English malcontents for more than a year, he accepted their invitation. Landing at Brixham on Tor Bay (November 5), he advanced slowly on London, as support fell away from James II. James's daughter Anne and his best general, John Churchill, were among the deserters to William's camp; thereupon James fled to France.

William was now asked to carry on the government and summon a Parliament. When this Convention Parliament met (Jan. 22, 1689), it agreed, after some debate, to treat James's flight as an abdication and to offer the crown, with

*An image of the landing of William of Orange, circa 1850.* Print Collector/
Hulton Archive/Getty Images

an accompanying Declaration of Right, to William and Mary
jointly. Both gift and conditions were accepted. Thereupon
the convention turned itself into a proper Parliament and
large parts of the Declaration into a Bill of Rights. This bill

gave the succession to Mary's sister, Anne, in default of issue to Mary; barred Roman Catholics from the throne; abolished the crown's power to suspend laws; condemned the power of dispensing with laws "as it hath been exercised and used of late"; and declared a standing army illegal in time of peace.

The settlement marked a considerable triumph for Whig views. If no Roman Catholic could be king, then no kingship could be unconditional. The adoption of the exclusionist solution lent support to John Locke's contention that government was in the nature of a social contract between the king and his people represented in parliament. The revolution permanently established Parliament as the ruling power of England.

## American Revolution

The American Revolution, also called the United States War of Independence or American Revolutionary War (1775–83), was an insurrection by which 13 of Great Britain's North American colonies won political independence and went on to form the United States of America. The war followed more than a decade of growing estrangement between the British crown and a large and influential segment of its North American colonies that was caused by British attempts to assert greater control over colonial affairs. Until early in 1778 the conflict was a civil war within the British Empire; afterward it became an international war as France (in 1778), Spain (in 1779), and the Netherlands (in 1780) joined the colonies against Britain. From the beginning sea power was vital in determining the course of the war, lending to British strategy a flexibility that helped compensate for the comparatively small numbers of troops sent to America and ultimately enabling the French to help bring about the final British surrender at Yorktown.

## Land Campaigns to 1778

Americans fought the war on land essentially with two types of organization, the Continental (national) Army and the state militias. The total number of the former provided by quotas from the states throughout the conflict was 231,771 men; the militias totaled 164,087. At any given time, however, the American forces seldom numbered over 20,000; in 1781 there were only about 29,000 insurgents under arms throughout the country. The war was therefore one fought by small field armies. Militias, poorly disciplined and with elected officers, were summoned for periods usually not exceeding three months. The terms of Continental Army service were only gradually increased from one to three years, and not even bounties and the offer of land kept the army up to strength. Reasons for the difficulty in maintaining an adequate Continental force included the colonists' traditional antipathy to regular armies, the objections of farmers to being away from their fields, the competition of the states with the Continental Congress to keep men in the militia, and the wretched and uncertain pay in a period of inflation.

By contrast, the British army was a reliable, steady force of professionals. Since it numbered only about 42,000, heavy recruiting programs were introduced. Many of the enlisted men were farm boys, as were most of the Americans. Others were unemployed persons from the urban slums. Still others joined the army to escape fines or imprisonment. The great majority became efficient soldiers owing to sound training and ferocious discipline. The officers were drawn largely from the gentry and the aristocracy and obtained their commissions and promotions by purchase. Though they received no formal training, they were not so dependent on a book knowledge of military tactics as were many of the Americans. British generals, however, tended toward a lack of imagination and initiative, while those who demonstrated such qualities often were rash.

Because troops were few and conscription unknown, the British government, following a traditional policy, purchased about 30,000 troops from various German princes. The Landgrave of Hesse furnished approximately three-fifths of this total. Few acts by the crown roused so much antagonism in America as this use of foreign mercenaries.

The war began in Massachusetts when Gen. Thomas Gage sent a force from Boston to destroy rebel military stores at Concord. Fighting occurred at Lexington and Concord on April 19, 1775, and only the arrival of reinforcements saved the British original column. Rebel militia then converged on Boston from all over New England. Their entrenching on Breed's Hill led to a British frontal assault on June 17 under Gen. William Howe, who won the hill but at the cost of more than 40 percent of the assault force.

Gen. George Washington was appointed commander in chief of the American forces by the Continental Congress. Not only did he have to contain the British in Boston but he also had to recruit a Continental army. During the winter of 1775–76 recruitment lagged so badly that fresh drafts of militia were called up to help maintain the siege. The balance shifted in late winter, when Gen. Henry Knox arrived with artillery from Fort Ticonderoga in New York, which had been captured from the British in May 1775. Mounted on Dorchester Heights, above Boston, the guns forced Howe, who had replaced Gage in command, to evacuate the city on March 17, 1776. Howe then repaired to Halifax to prepare for an invasion of New York, and Washington moved units southward for its defense.

Meanwhile, action flared in the north. In the fall of 1775 the Americans invaded Canada. One force under Gen. Richard Montgomery captured Montreal on November 13.

An image of the Battle of Monmouth, depicting George Washington leading the American attack on British troops during the American Revolutionary War. Stock Montage/Archive Photos/Getty Images

Another under Benedict Arnold made a remarkable march through the Maine wilderness to Quebec. Unable to take the city, Arnold was presently joined by Montgomery, many of whose troops had gone home because their enlistments had expired. An attack on the city on the last day of the year failed, Montgomery was killed, and many troops were captured. The Americans maintained a siege of the city but withdrew with the arrival of British reinforcements in the spring. Pursued by the British and decimated by smallpox, the Americans fell back to Ticonderoga. Gen. Guy Carleton's hopes of moving quickly down Lake Champlain, however, were frustrated by Arnold's construction of a fighting fleet. Forced to build one of his own, Carleton destroyed most of the American fleet in October 1776 but considered the season too advanced to bring Ticonderoga under siege.

As the Americans suffered defeat in Canada, so did the British in the South. North Carolina patriots trounced a body of loyalists at Moore's Creek Bridge on Feb. 27, 1776. Charleston, S.C., was successfully defended against a British assault by sea in June.

Having made up its mind to crush the rebellion, the British government sent General Howe and his brother, Richard, Admiral Lord Howe, with a large fleet and 34,000 British and German troops to New York. It also gave the Howes a commission to treat with the Americans. The Continental Congress, which had proclaimed the independence of the colonies, at first thought the Howes empowered to negotiate peace terms but discovered that they were authorized only to accept submission and assure pardons.

Their peace efforts getting nowhere, the Howes turned to force. Under his brother's guns, General Howe landed troops on Long Island and on August 27 scored a smashing victory. Washington evacuated his army from Brooklyn to Manhattan that night under cover of a fog. On September

15, Howe followed up his victory by invading Manhattan. Though checked at Harlem Heights the next day, he drew Washington off the island in October by a move to Throg's Neck and then to New Rochelle, northeast of the city. Leaving garrisons at Fort Washington on Manhattan and at Fort Lee on the opposite shore of the Hudson River, Washington hastened to block Howe. The latter, however, defeated him on October 28 at Chatterton Hill near White Plains. Howe slipped between the American army and Fort Washington and stormed the fort on November 16, seizing nearly 3,000 prisoners, guns, and supplies. British forces under Lord Cornwallis then took Fort Lee and on November 24 started to drive the American army across New Jersey. Though Washington escaped to the west bank of the Delaware River, his army nearly disappeared. Howe then put his army into winter quarters, with outposts at towns such as Bordentown and Trenton.

On Christmas night Washington struck back with a brilliant riposte. Crossing the ice-strewn Delaware with 2,400 men, he fell upon the Hessian garrison at Trenton at dawn and took nearly 1,000 prisoners. Though almost trapped by Cornwallis, who recovered Trenton on Jan. 2, 1777, Washington made a skillful escape during the night, won a battle against British reinforcements at Princeton the next day, and went into winter quarters in the defensible area around Morristown. The Trenton-Princeton campaign roused the country and saved the struggle for independence from collapse.

Britain's strategy in 1777 aimed at driving a wedge between New England and the other colonies. An army under Gen. John Burgoyne was to march south from Canada and join forces with Howe on the Hudson. But Howe seems to have concluded that Burgoyne was strong enough to operate on his own and left New York in the summer, taking his army by sea to the head of Chesapeake Bay. Once ashore, he

*The painting* Washington Crossing the Delaware, *by Emanuel Leutze, depicts Gen. George Washington crossing the Delaware River from Pennsylvania to New Jersey on Dec. 25, 1776.* Time & Life Pictures/Getty Images

defeated Washington badly but not decisively at Brandywine Creek on September 11. Then, feinting westward, he entered Philadelphia, the American capital, on September 25. The Continental Congress fled to York. Washington struck back at Germantown on October 4 but, compelled to withdraw, went into winter quarters at Valley Forge.

In the north the story was different. Burgoyne was to move south to Albany with a force of about 9,000 British, Germans, Indians, and American loyalists; a smaller force under Lt. Col. Barry St. Leger was to converge on Albany through the Mohawk valley. Burgoyne took Ticonderoga handily on July 5 and then, instead of using Lake George, chose a southward route by land. Slowed by the rugged terrain, strewn with trees cut down by American axmen under Gen. Philip Schuyler, and needing horses, Burgoyne sent a force of Germans to collect them at Bennington, Vt. The Germans were nearly wiped out on August 16 by New Englanders under Gen. John Stark and Col. Seth Warner. Meanwhile, St. Leger besieged Fort Schuyler (present Rome, N.Y.), ambushed a relief column of American militia at Oriskany on August 6, but retreated as his Indians gave up the siege and an American force under Arnold approached. Burgoyne himself reached the Hudson, but the Americans, now under Gen. Horatio Gates, checked him at Freeman's Farm on September 19 and, thanks to Arnold's battlefield leadership, decisively defeated him at Bemis Heights on October 7. Ten days later, unable to get help from New York, Burgoyne surrendered at Saratoga.

The most significant result of Burgoyne's capitulation was the entrance of France into the war. The French had secretly furnished financial and material aid since 1776. Now they prepared fleets and armies, although they did not formally declare war until June 1778.

## Land Campaigns from 1778

Meanwhile, the Americans at Valley Forge survived a hungry winter, which was made worse by quartermaster and commissary mismanagement, graft of contractors, and unwillingness of farmers to sell produce for paper money. Order and discipline among the troops were improved by the arrival of the Freiherr von (baron of) Steuben, a Prussian officer in the service of France. Steuben instituted a training program in which he emphasized drilling by officers, marching in column, and using firearms more effectively.

The program paid off at Monmouth Court House, N.J., on June 28, 1778, when Washington attacked the British, who were withdrawing from Philadelphia to New York. Although

Sir Henry Clinton, who had replaced Howe, struck back hard, the Americans stood their ground.

French aid now materialized with the appearance of a strong fleet under the comte d'Estaing. Unable to enter New York harbour, d'Estaing tried to assist Maj. Gen. John Sullivan in dislodging the British from Newport, R.I. Storms and British reinforcements thwarted the joint effort.

Action in the North was largely a stalemate for the rest of the war. The British raided New Bedford, Mass., and New Haven and New London, Conn., while loyalists and Indians attacked settlements in New York and Pennsylvania. On the other hand, the Americans under Anthony Wayne stormed Stony Point, N.Y., on July 16, 1779, and "Light-Horse Harry" Lee took Paulus Hook, N.J., on August 19. More lasting in effect was Sullivan's expedition of August 1779 against Britain's Indian allies in New York, particularly the destruction of their villages and fields of corn. Farther west, Col. George Rogers Clark seized Vincennes and other posts north of the Ohio River in 1778.

Potentially serious blows to the American cause were Arnold's defection in 1780 and the army mutinies of 1780 and 1781. Arnold's attempt to betray West Point to the British miscarried. Mutinies were sparked by misunderstandings over terms of enlistment, poor food and clothing, gross arrears of pay, and the decline in the purchasing power of the dollar. Suppressed by force or negotiation, the mutinies shook the morale of the army.

The Americans also suffered setbacks in the South. British strategy from 1778 called for offensives that were designed to take advantage of the flexibility of sea power and the loyalist sentiment of many of the people. British forces from New York and St. Augustine, Fla., occupied Georgia by the end of January 1779 and successfully defended Savannah in the fall against d'Estaing and a Franco-American army. Clinton, having withdrawn his Newport garrison, captured Charleston—and an American army of 5,000 under Gen. Benjamin Lincoln—in May 1780. Learning that Newport was threatened by a French expeditionary force under the comte de Rochambeau, Clinton returned to New York, leaving Cornwallis at Charleston.

Cornwallis, however, took the offensive. On August 16 he shattered General Gates's army at Camden, S.C. The destruction of a force of loyalists at Kings Mountain on October 7 led him to move against the new American commander, Gen. Nathanael Greene. When Greene put part of his force under Gen. Daniel Morgan, Cornwallis sent his cavalry leader, Col. Banastre Tarleton, after Morgan. At Cowpens on Jan. 17, 1781, Morgan destroyed practically all of Tarleton's column. Subsequently, on March 15, Greene and Cornwallis fought at Guilford Courthouse, N.C. Cornwallis won but suffered heavy casualties. After withdrawing to Wilmington, he marched into Virginia to join British forces sent there by Clinton.

Greene then moved back to South Carolina, where he was defeated by Lord Rawdon at Hobkirk's Hill on April 25 and at Ninety-Six in June and by Lt. Col. Alexander Stewart at Eutaw Springs on September 8. In spite of this, the British, harassed by partisan leaders such as Francis Marion, Thomas Sumter, and Andrew Pickens, soon retired to the coast and remained locked up in Charleston and Savannah.

Meanwhile, Cornwallis entered Virginia. Sending Tarleton on raids across the state, he started to build a base at Yorktown, at the same time fending off American forces under Wayne, Steuben, and the marquis de Lafayette.

Learning that the comte de Grasse had arrived in the Chesapeake with a large fleet and 3,000 French troops, Washington and Rochambeau moved south to Virginia.

By mid-September the Franco-American forces had placed Yorktown under siege, and British rescue efforts proved fruitless. Cornwallis surrendered his army of more than 7,000 men on October 19. Thus, for the second time during the war the British had lost an entire army.

Thereafter, land action in America died out, though the war persisted in other theatres and on the high seas. Eventually Clinton was replaced by Sir Guy Carleton. While the peace treaties were under consideration and afterward, Carleton evacuated thousands of loyalists from America, including many from Savannah on July 11, 1782, and others from Charleston on December 14. The last British forces finally left New York on Nov. 25, 1783. Washington then reentered the city in triumph.

## The War at Sea

Although the colonists ventured to challenge Britain's naval power from the outbreak of the conflict, the war at sea in its later stages was fought mainly between Britain and America's European allies, the American effort being reduced to privateering.

The importance of sea power was recognized early. In October 1775 the Continental Congress authorized the creation of the Continental Navy and established the Marine Corps in November. The navy, taking its direction from the naval and marine committees of the Congress, was only occasionally effective. In 1776 it had 27 ships against Britain's 270; by the end of the war, the British total had risen close to 500, and the American had dwindled to 20. Many of the best seamen available went off privateering, and both Continental Navy commanders and crews suffered from a lack of training and discipline.

The first significant blow by the navy was struck by Cdre. Esek Hopkins, who captured New Providence (Nassau) in the Bahamas in 1776.

Other captains, such as Lambert Wickes, Gustavus Conyngham, and John Barry, also enjoyed successes, but the Scottish-born John Paul Jones was especially notable. As captain of the *Ranger*, Jones scourged the British coasts in 1778, capturing the man-of-war *Drake*. As captain of the *Bonhomme Richard* in 1779, he intercepted a timber convoy and captured the British frigate *Serapis*.

More injurious to the British were the raids by American privateers on their shipping. American ships, furnished with letters of marque by the Congress or the states, swarmed about the British Isles. By the end of 1777 they had taken 560 British vessels, and by the end of the war they had probably seized 1,500. More than 12,000 British sailors also were captured. One result was that, by 1781, British merchants were clamouring for an end to hostilities.

Most of the naval action occurred at sea. The significant exceptions were Arnold's battles against General Carleton's fleet on Lake Champlain at Valcour Island on October 11 and off Split Rock on October 13, 1776. Arnold lost both battles, but his construction of a fleet of tiny vessels, mostly gondolas (gundalows) and galleys, had forced the British to build a larger fleet and hence delayed their attack on Fort Ticonderoga until the following spring. This delay contributed significantly to Burgoyne's capitulation in October 1777.

The entrance of France into the war, followed by that of Spain in 1779 and the Netherlands in 1780, effected important changes in the naval aspect of the war. The Spanish and Dutch were not particularly active, but their role in keeping British naval forces tied down in Europe was significant. The British navy could not maintain an effective blockade of both the American coast and the enemies' ports. Owing to years of economy and neglect, Britain's ships of the line were neither modern nor sufficiently numerous. An immediate result was that France's Toulon fleet under d'Estaing got safely away to America, where it appeared off New York and later assisted General Sullivan in the unsuccessful siege of Newport. A fierce battle off Ushant, France, in July 1778 between the Channel fleet under Adm. Augustus Keppel and the Brest fleet under the comte d'Orvilliers proved inconclusive. Had Keppel won decisively, French aid to the Americans would have diminished and Rochambeau might never have been able to lead his expedition to America.

In the following year England was in real danger. Not only did it have to face the privateers of the United States, France, and Spain off its coasts, as well as the raids of John Paul Jones, but it also lived in fear of invasion. The combined fleets of France and Spain had acquired command of the Channel, and a French army of 50,000 waited for the propitious moment to board their transports. Luckily for the British, storms, sickness among the allied crews, and changes of plans terminated the threat.

Despite allied supremacy in the Channel in 1779, the threat of invasion, and the loss of islands in the West Indies, the British maintained control of the North American seaboard for most of 1779 and 1780, which made possible their southern land campaigns. They also reinforced Gibraltar, which the Spaniards had brought under siege in the fall of 1779, and sent a fleet under Admiral Sir George Rodney to the West Indies in early 1780. After fruitless maneuvering against the comte de Guichen, who had replaced d'Estaing, Rodney sailed for New York.

While Rodney had been in the West Indies, a French squadron slipped out of Brest and sailed to Newport with Rochambeau's army. Rodney, instead of trying to block the approach to Newport, returned to the West Indies, where, upon receiving instructions to attack Dutch possessions, he seized Sint Eustatius, the Dutch island that served as the principal depot for war materials shipped from Europe and transshipped into American vessels. He became so involved in the disposal of the enormous booty that he dallied at the island for six months.

In the meantime, a powerful British fleet relieved Gibraltar in 1781, but the price was the departure of the French fleet at Brest, part of it to India, the larger part under Admiral de Grasse to the West Indies. After maneuvering indecisively against Rodney, de Grasse received a request from Washington and Rochambeau to come to New York or the Chesapeake.

Earlier, in March, a French squadron had tried to bring troops from Newport to the Chesapeake but was forced to return by Adm. Marriot Arbuthnot, who had succeeded Lord Howe. Soon afterward Arbuthnot was replaced by Thomas Graves, a conventional-minded admiral.

Informed that a French squadron would shortly leave the West Indies, Rodney sent Samuel Hood north with a powerful force while he sailed for England, taking with him several formidable ships that might better have been left with Hood.

Soon after Hood dropped anchor in New York, de Grasse appeared in the Chesapeake, where he landed troops to help Lafayette contain Cornwallis until Washington and Rochambeau could arrive. Fearful that the comte de Barras, who was carrying Rochambeau's artillery train from Newport, might join de Grasse, and hoping to intercept him, Graves sailed with Hood to the Chesapeake. Graves had 19 ships of the line against de Grasse's 24. Though the battle that began on September 5 off the Virginia capes was not a skillfully managed affair, Graves had the worst of it and retired to New York. He ventured out again on October 17 with a strong contingent of troops and 25 ships of the line, while de Grasse, reinforced by Barras, now had 36 ships of the line. No battle occurred, however, when Graves learned that Cornwallis had surrendered.

Although Britain subsequently recouped some of its fortunes, by Rodney defeating and capturing de Grasse in the Battle of the Saints off Dominica in 1782 and British land and sea forces inflicting defeats in India, the turn of events did not significantly alter the situation in America as it existed after Yorktown. A new government under Lord Shelburne tried to get the American commissioners to agree to a separate peace, but, ultimately, the treaty negotiated with the Americans was not to go into effect until the formal conclusion of a peace with their European allies.

## Aftermath

The Peace of Paris (Sept. 3, 1783) ended the U.S. War of Independence. Great Britain recognized the independence of the United States (with western boundaries to the Mississippi River) and ceded Florida to Spain. Other provisions called for payment of U.S. private debts to British citizens, American use of the Newfoundland fisheries, and fair treatment for American colonials loyal to Britain.

In explaining the outcome of the war, scholars have pointed out that the British never contrived an overall general strategy for winning it. Also, even if the war could have been terminated by British power in the early stages, the generals during that period, notably Howe, declined to make a prompt, vigorous, intelligent application of that power. They acted, to be sure, within the conventions of their age, but in choosing to take minimal risks (for example, Carleton at Ticonderoga and Howe at Brooklyn Heights and later in New Jersey and Pennsylvania) they lost the opportunity to deal potentially mortal blows to the rebellion. There was also a grave lack of understanding and cooperation at crucial moments (as with Burgoyne and Howe in 1777). Finally, the British counted too strongly on loyalist support they did not receive.

But British mistakes alone could not account for the success of the United States. Feeble as their war effort occasionally became, the Americans were able generally to take advantage of their enemies' mistakes. The Continental Army, moreover, was by no means an inept force even before Steuben's reforms. The militias, while usually unreliable, could perform admirably under the leadership of men who understood them, like Arnold, Greene, and Morgan, and often reinforced the Continentals in crises. Furthermore, Washington, a rock in adversity, learned slowly but reasonably well the art of generalship. The supplies and funds furnished by France from 1776 to 1778 were invaluable, while French military and naval support after 1778 was essential. The outcome, therefore, resulted from a combination of British blunders, American efforts, and French assistance.

## French Revolution

The French Revolution, also called the Revolution of 1789, was the revolutionary movement that shook France between 1787 and 1799 and reached its first climax there in 1789. Hence the conventional term "Revolution of 1789," denoting the end of the *ancien régime* in France and serving also to distinguish that event from the later French revolutions of 1830 and 1848.

Although historians disagree on the causes of the Revolution, the following reasons are commonly adduced: (1) the increasingly prosperous elite of wealthy commoners— merchants, manufacturers, and professionals, often called the bourgeoisie—produced by the 18th century's economic growth resented its exclusion from political power and positions of honour; (2) the peasants were acutely aware of their situation and were less and less willing to support the anachronistic and burdensome feudal system; (3) the *philosophes*, who advocated social and political reform, had been read more widely in France than anywhere else; (4) French participation in the American Revolution had driven the government to the brink of bankruptcy; and (5) crop failures in much of the country in 1788, coming on top of a long period of economic difficulties, made the population particularly restless.

## Aristocratic Revolt, 1787–89

The Revolution took shape in France when the controller general of finances, Charles-Alexandre de Calonne, arranged the summoning of an assembly of "notables" (prelates, great noblemen, and a few representatives of the bourgeoisie) in February 1787 to propose reforms designed to eliminate the budget deficit by increasing the taxation of the privileged classes. The assembly refused to take responsibility for the reforms and suggested the calling of the Estates-General, which represented the clergy, the nobility, and the Third Estate (the commoners) and which had not met since 1614. The efforts made by Calonne's successors to enforce fiscal reforms in spite of resistance by the privileged classes led to the so-called revolt of the "aristocratic bodies," notably that of the *parlements* (the most important courts of justice), whose powers were curtailed by the edict of May 1788. During the spring and summer of 1788, there was unrest among the populace in Paris, Grenoble, Dijon, Toulouse, Pau, and Rennes. The king, Louis XVI, had to yield; reappointing reform-minded Jacques Necker as the finance minister, he promised to convene the Estates-General on May 5, 1789. He also, in practice, granted freedom of the press, and France was flooded with pamphlets addressing the reconstruction of the state. The elections to the Estates-General, held between January and April 1789, coincided with further disturbances, as the harvest of 1788 had been a bad one. There were practically no exclusions from the voting; and the electors drew up *cahiers de doléances*, which listed their grievances and hopes. They elected 600 deputies for the Third Estate, 300 for the nobility, and 300 for the clergy.

## Events of 1789

The Estates-General met at Versailles on May 5, 1789. They were immediately divided over a fundamental issue: should they vote by head, giving the advantage to the Third Estate, or by estate, in which case the two privileged orders of the realm might outvote the third? On June 17 the bitter struggle over this legal issue finally drove the deputies of the Third Estate to declare themselves the National Assembly; they threatened to proceed, if necessary, without the other two orders. They were supported by many of the parish priests, who outnumbered the aristocratic upper clergy among the church's deputies. When royal officials locked the deputies out of their regular meeting hall on June 20, they occupied the king's indoor tennis court (*jeu de paume*) and swore an oath not to disperse until they had given France a new constitution. The king grudgingly gave in and urged the nobles and the remaining clergy to join the assembly, which took the official title of National Constituent Assembly on July 9; at the same time, however, he began gathering troops to dissolve it.

These two months of prevarication at a time when the problem of maintaining food supplies had reached its climax infuriated the towns and the provinces. Rumours of an "aristocratic conspiracy" by the king and the privileged to overthrow the Third Estate led to the Great Fear of July 1789, when the peasants were nearly panic-stricken. The gathering of troops around Paris and the dismissal of Necker provoked insurrection in the capital. On July 14, 1789, the Parisian crowd seized the Bastille, a symbol of royal tyranny. Again the king had to yield; visiting Paris, he showed his recognition of the sovereignty of the people by wearing the tricolour cockade.

In the provinces, the Great Fear of July led the peasants to rise against their lords. The nobles and the bourgeois now took fright. The National Constituent Assembly could see only one way to check the peasants; on the night of Aug. 4, 1789, it decreed the abolition of the feudal regime and of the tithe. Then on August 26 it introduced the Declaration of the Rights of Man and of the Citizen, proclaiming liberty, equality, the inviolability of property, and the right to resist oppression.

The decrees of August 4 and the Declaration were such innovations that the king refused to sanction them. The Parisians rose again and on October 5 marched to Versailles. The next day they brought the royal family back to Paris. The National Constituent Assembly followed the court, and in Paris it continued to work on the new constitution.

The French population participated actively in the new political culture created by the Revolution. Dozens of uncensored newspapers kept citizens abreast of events, and political clubs allowed them to voice their opinions. Public ceremonies such as the planting of "trees of liberty" in small villages and the Festival of Federation, held in Paris in 1790 on the first anniversary of the storming of the Bastille, were symbolic affirmations of the new order.

## The New Regime

The National Constituent Assembly completed the abolition of feudalism, suppressed the old "orders," established civil equality among men (at least in metropolitan France, since slavery was retained in the colonies), and made more than half the adult male population eligible to vote, although only a small minority met the requirement for becoming a deputy. The decision to nationalize the lands of the Roman Catholic Church in France to pay off the public debt led to a widespread redistribution of property. The bourgeoisie and the peasant landowners were undoubtedly the chief beneficiaries, but some farm workers also were able to buy land. Having deprived the church of its resources, the assembly then resolved to reorganize the church, enacting the Civil Constitution of the Clergy, which was rejected by the pope and by many of the French clergy. This produced a schism that aggravated the violence of the accompanying controversies.

The complicated administrative system of the *ancien régime* was swept away by the National Constituent Assembly, which substituted a rational system based on the division of France into *départements*, districts, cantons, and communes administered by elected assemblies. The principles underlying the administration of justice were also radically changed, and the system was adapted to the new administrative divisions. Significantly, the judges were to be elected.

The National Constituent Assembly tried to create a monarchical regime in which the legislative and executive powers were shared between the king and an assembly. This regime might have worked if the king had really wanted to govern with the new authorities, but Louis XVI was weak and vacillating and was the prisoner of his aristocratic advisers. On June 20–21, 1791, he tried to flee the country, but he was stopped at Varennes and brought back to Paris.

## Counterrevolution, Regicide, and the Reign of Terror

The events in France gave new hope to the revolutionaries who had been defeated a few years previously in the United Provinces, Belgium, and Switzerland. Likewise, all those who wanted changes in England, Ireland, the German states, the Austrian lands, or Italy looked upon the Revolution with sympathy.

A number of French counterrevolutionaries—nobles, ecclesiastics, and some bourgeois—abandoned the struggle in their own country and emigrated. As "émigrés," many formed armed groups close to the northeastern frontier of France and sought help from the rulers of Europe. The rulers were at first indifferent to the Revolution but began to worry when the National Constituent Assembly proclaimed a revolutionary principle of international law—namely, that a people had the right of self-determination. In accordance with this principle, the papal territory of Avignon was reunited with France on Sept. 13, 1791. By early 1792 both radicals, eager to spread the principles of the Revolution, and the king, hopeful that war would either strengthen his authority or allow foreign armies to rescue him, supported an aggressive policy. France declared war against Austria on April 20, 1792.

In the first phase of the war (April–September 1792), France suffered defeats; Prussia joined the war in July, and an Austro-Prussian army crossed the frontier and advanced rapidly toward Paris. Believing that they had been betrayed by the king and the aristocrats, the Paris revolutionaries rose on Aug. 10, 1792, occupied Tuileries Palace, where Louis XVI was living, and imprisoned the royal family in the Temple. At the beginning of September, the Parisian crowd broke into the prisons and massacred the nobles and clergy held there. Meanwhile, volunteers were pouring into the army as the Revolution had awakened French nationalism. In a final effort the French forces checked the Prussians on Sept. 20, 1792, at Valmy. On the same day, a new assembly, the National Convention, met. The next day it proclaimed the abolition of the monarchy and the establishment of the republic.

In the second phase of the war (September 1792–April 1793), the revolutionaries got the better of the enemy. Belgium, the Rhineland, Savoy, and the county of Nice were occupied by French armies. Meanwhile, the National Convention was divided between the Girondins, who wanted to organize a bourgeois republic in France and to spread the Revolution over the whole of Europe, and the Montagnards ("Mountain Men"), who, with Maximillian Robespierre, wanted to give the lower classes a greater share in political and economic power. Despite efforts made by the Girondins, Louis XVI was judged by the Convention, condemned to death for treason, and executed on Jan. 21, 1793; the queen, Marie-Antoinette, was guillotined nine months later.

In the spring of 1793, the war entered a third phase, marked by new French defeats. Austria, Prussia, and Great Britain formed a coalition (later called the First Coalition), to which most of the rulers of Europe adhered. France lost Belgium and the Rhineland, and invading forces threatened Paris. These reverses, as those of 1792 had done, strengthened the extremists. The Girondin leaders were driven from the National Convention, and the Montagnards, who had the support of the Paris *sansculottes* (workers, craftsmen, and shopkeepers), seized power and kept it until 9 Thermidor, year II, of the new French republican calendar (July 27, 1794). The Montagnards were bourgeois liberals like the Girondins but under pressure from the *sansculottes*, and, in order to meet the requirements of defense, they adopted a radical economic and social policy. They introduced the Maximum (government control of prices), taxed the rich, brought national assistance to the poor and to the disabled, declared that education should be free and compulsory, and ordered the confiscation and sale of the property of émigrés. These exceptional measures provoked violent reactions: the Wars of the Vendée, the "federalist" risings in Normandy and in Provence, the revolts of Lyon and Bordeaux, and the insurrection of the Chouans in Brittany. Opposition, however, was broken by the Reign of Terror (19 Fructidor, year I–9 Thermidor, year II [Sept. 5, 1793–July 27, 1794]), which entailed the arrest of at least 300,000 suspects, 17,000 of whom were sentenced to death and executed while more died in prisons or were killed without any form of trial. At the same time, the revolutionary government raised an army of more than one million men.

Thanks to this army, the war entered its fourth phase (beginning in the spring of 1794). A brilliant victory over the Austrians at Fleurus on 8 Messidor, year II (June 26, 1794), enabled the French to reoccupy Belgium. Victory made the Terror and the economic and social restrictions seem pointless. Robespierre, "the Incorruptible," who had sponsored the restrictions, was overthrown in the National Convention on 9 Thermidor, year II (July 27, 1794), and executed the following day. Soon after his fall the Maximum was abolished, the social laws were no longer applied, and efforts toward economic equality were abandoned. Reaction set in; the National Convention began to debate a new constitution; and, meanwhile, in the west and in the southeast, a royalist "White Terror" broke out. Royalists even tried to seize power in Paris but were crushed by the young general Napoleon Bonaparte on 13 Vendémiaire, year IV (Oct. 5, 1795). A few days later the National Convention dispersed.

## The Directory and Revolutionary Expansion

The constitution of the year III, which the National Convention had approved, placed executive power in a Directory of five members and legislative power in two chambers, the Council of Ancients and the Council of the Five Hundred (together called the Corps Législatif). This regime, a bourgeois republic, might have achieved stability had not war perpetuated the struggle between revolutionaries and counterrevolutionaries throughout Europe. The war, moreover, embittered existing antagonisms between the Directory and the legislative councils in France and often gave rise to new ones. These disputes were settled by coups d'état, chiefly those of 18 Fructidor, year V (Sept. 4, 1797), which removed the royalists from the Directory and from the councils, and of 18 Brumaire, year VIII (Nov. 9, 1799), in which Bonaparte abolished the Directory and became the leader of France as its "first consul."

After the victory of Fleurus, the progress of the French armies in Europe had continued. The Rhineland and Holland were occupied, and in 1795 Holland, Tuscany, Prussia, and Spain negotiated for peace. When the French army under Bonaparte entered Italy (1796), Sardinia came quickly to terms. Austria was the last to give in (Treaty of Campo Formio, 1797). Most of the countries occupied by the French were organized as "sister republics," with institutions modeled on those of Revolutionary France.

Peace on the continent of Europe, however, did not end revolutionary expansion. The majority of the directors had inherited the Girondin desire to spread the Revolution over Europe and listened to the appeals of Jacobins abroad. Thus French troops in 1798 and 1799 entered Switzerland, the Papal States, and Naples and set up the Helvetic, Roman, and Parthenopean republics. Great Britain, however, remained at war with France. Unable to effect a landing in England, the Directory, on Bonaparte's request, decided to threaten the British in India by occupying Egypt. An expeditionary corps under Bonaparte easily occupied Malta and Egypt, but the squadron that had convoyed it was destroyed by Horatio

*Napoleon Bonaparte.* Imagno/Hulton Fine Art Collection/Getty Images

Nelson's fleet at the Battle of the Nile on 14 Thermidor, year VI (Aug. 1, 1798). This disaster encouraged the formation of a Second Coalition of powers alarmed by the progress of the Revolution. This coalition of Austria, Russia, Turkey, and Great Britain won great successes during the spring and summer of 1799 and drove back the French armies to the frontiers. Bonaparte thereupon returned to France to exploit his own great prestige and the disrepute into which the military reverses had brought the government. His coup d'état of 18 Brumaire overthrew the Directory and substituted the consulate. Although Bonaparte proclaimed the end of the Revolution, he himself was to spread it in new forms throughout Europe.

## Arab Spring

The Arab Spring was a wave of pro-democracy protests and uprisings that took place in the Middle East and North Africa beginning in 2010 and 2011, challenging some of the region's entrenched authoritarian regimes. Demonstrators expressing political and economic grievances faced violent crackdowns by their countries' security forces.

In January and February 2011, protests in Tunisia and Egypt succeeded in a matter of weeks in toppling two regimes thought to be among the region's most stable. The first demonstrations took place in central Tunisia in December 2010, catalyzed by the self-immolation of Mohamed Bouazizi, a 26-year-old street vendor protesting his treatment by local officials. A protest movement, dubbed the "Jasmine Revolution" in the media, quickly spread through the country. The Tunisian government attempted to end the unrest by using violence against street demonstrations and by offering political and economic concessions. However, protests soon overwhelmed the country's security forces, compelling Pres.

*Residents of Sidi Bouzid, Tunisia, during a demonstration on Dec. 27, 2010.*
Fethi Belaid/AFP/Getty Images

Zine al-Abidine Ben Ali to step down and flee the country in January 2011. In October 2011, Tunisians participated in a free election to choose members of a council tasked with drafting a new constitution. A democratically chosen president and prime minister took office in December 2011.

Massive protests broke out in Egypt in late January 2011, only days after Ben Ali's ouster in Tunisia. The Egyptian government also tried and failed to control protests by offering concessions while cracking down violently against protesters. After several days of massive demonstrations and clashes between protesters and security forces in Cairo and around the country, a turning point came at the end of the month when the Egyptian army announced that it would refuse to use force against protesters calling for the removal of Pres. Ḥosnī Mubārak. Having lost the support of the military, Mubārak left office on February 11 after nearly 30 years, ceding power to a council of senior military officers.

In the period of euphoria that followed, the new military administration enjoyed high public approval, since the military had played a decisive role in ending the Mubārak regime. However, optimism was dampened when the new administration appeared hesitant to begin a full transfer of power to an elected government and when military and security forces resumed the use of violence against protesters. Confrontations between protesters and security forces became frequent occurrences. In spite of a multiday outbreak of violence in late November 2011, parliamentary elections proceeded as scheduled and the newly elected People's Assembly held its inaugural session in late January 2012.

Encouraged by protesters' rapid successes in Tunisia and Egypt, protest movements took hold in Yemen, Bahrain, Libya, and Syria in late January, February, and March 2011. In these countries, however, outpourings of popular discontent led to protracted bloody struggles between opposition groups and ruling regimes.

In Yemen, where the first protests appeared in late January 2011, Pres. ʿAlī ʿAbd Allāh Ṣāliḥ's base of support was damaged when a number of the country's most powerful tribal and military leaders aligned themselves with the pro-democracy protesters calling for him to step down. When negotiations to remove Ṣāliḥ from power failed, loyalist and opposition fighters clashed in Sanaa. Ṣāliḥ left Yemen in June to receive medical treatment after he was injured in a bomb attack, raising hopes among the opposition that a transition would begin. Ṣāliḥ returned to the country unexpectedly four months later, however, adding to the uncertainty and confusion about Yemen's political future. In November 2011 Ṣāliḥ signed an internationally mediated agreement calling for a phased transfer of power to the vice president, 'Abd Rabbuh Manṣūr Hadī. In accordance with the agreement, Hadī took over governing responsibility immediately and formally assumed the presidency after standing as the sole candidate in a presidential election in February 2012.

Mass protests demanding political and economic reforms erupted in Bahrain in mid-February 2011, led by Bahraini human rights activists and members of Bahrain's marginalized Shī'ite majority. Protests were violently suppressed by Bahraini security forces, aided by a force of about 1,500 soldiers from Saudi Arabia and the United Arab Emirates that entered the country in March. By the end of the month, the mass protest movement had been stifled. In the aftermath of the protests, dozens of accused protest leaders were convicted of antigovernment activity and imprisoned, hundreds of Shī'ite workers suspected of supporting the protests were fired, and dozens of Shī'ite mosques were demolished by the government. In November 2011 an independent investigation into the uprising, commissioned by the Bahraini government, concluded that the government had used excessive force and torture against protesters. The government vowed to act on the recommendations for reform included in the report.

In Libya protests against the regime of Muammar al-Qaddafi in mid-February 2011 quickly escalated into an armed revolt. When the rebel forces appeared to be on the verge of defeat in March, an international coalition led by NATO launched a campaign of air strikes targeting Qaddafi's forces. Although NATO intervention ultimately shifted the military balance in favour of the rebel forces, Qaddafi was able to cling to power in the capital, Tripoli, for several more months. He was forced from power in August 2011 after rebel forces took control of Tripoli. After evading capture for several weeks, Qaddafi was killed in Surt in October 2011 as rebel forces took control of the city.

The challenges of governing Libya in the post-Qaddafi era became apparent soon after the internationally recognized provisional government, known as the Transitional National Council (TNC), took power. The TNC struggled to restart the Libyan economy, establish functional institutions of government, and exert control over the many autonomous regional and tribal militias that had participated in the rebellion against Qaddafi.

In Syria protests calling for the resignation of Pres. Bashar al-Assad broke out in southern Syria in mid-March 2011 and spread through the country. The Assad regime responded with a brutal crackdown against protesters, drawing condemnation from international leaders and human rights groups. A leadership council for the Syrian opposition formed in Istanbul in August, and opposition militias began to launch attacks on government forces. In spite of the upheaval, Assad's hold on power appeared strong, as he was able to retain the support of critical military units composed largely of members of Syria's 'Alawite minority, to which Assad also belonged. Meanwhile, divisions in the international community made it unlikely that international military intervention, which had proved decisive in Libya, would be possible in Syria. Russia and China vetoed UN Security Council resolutions meant to pressure the Assad regime in October 2011 and February 2012 and vowed to oppose any measure that would lead to foreign intervention in Syria or Assad's removal from power. The arrival of a delegation of peace monitors from the Arab League in December 2011 did little to reduce violence. The monitoring mission was suspended several weeks later over concerns for the safety of the monitors.

The effects of the Arab Spring movement were felt elsewhere throughout the Middle East and North Africa as many of the countries in the region experienced at least minor pro-democracy protests. In Algeria, Jordan, Morocco, and Oman, rulers offered a variety of concessions, ranging from the dismissal of unpopular officials to constitutional changes, in order to head off the spread of protest movements in their countries.

# CHAPTER 3

# TERRORISM

Terrorism is the systematic use of violence to create a general climate of fear in a population and thereby to bring about a particular political objective. Terrorism has been practiced by political organizations with both rightist and leftist objectives, by nationalistic and religious groups, by revolutionaries, and even by state institutions such as armies, intelligence services, and police.

Definitions of terrorism are usually complex and controversial, and, because of the inherent ferocity and violence of terrorism, the term in its popular usage has developed an intense stigma. It was first coined in the 1790s to refer to the terror used during the French Revolution by the revolutionaries against their opponents. The Jacobin party of Maximilien Robespierre carried out a Reign of Terror involving mass executions by the guillotine. Although terrorism in this usage implies an act of violence by a state against its domestic enemies, since the 20th century the term has been applied most frequently to violence aimed, either directly or indirectly, at governments in an effort to influence policy or topple an existing regime.

Terrorism is not legally defined in all jurisdictions; the statutes that do exist, however, generally share some common elements. Terrorism involves the use or threat of violence and seeks to create fear, not just within the direct victims but among a wide audience. The degree to which

*Painting of the execution by guillotine of Louis XVI of France on Jan. 21, 1793.* Universal Images Group/Getty Images

it relies on fear distinguishes terrorism from both conventional and guerrilla warfare. Although conventional military forces invariably engage in psychological warfare against the enemy, their principal means of victory is strength of arms. Similarly, guerrilla forces, which often rely on acts of terror and other forms of propaganda, aim at military victory and occasionally succeed (e.g., the Viet Cong in Vietnam and the Khmer Rouge in Cambodia). Terrorism proper is thus the systematic use of violence to generate fear, and thereby to achieve political goals, when direct military victory is not possible. This has led some social scientists to refer to guerrilla warfare as the "weapon of the weak" and terrorism as the "weapon of the weakest."

In order to attract and maintain the publicity necessary to generate widespread fear, terrorists must engage in increasingly dramatic, violent, and high-profile attacks. These have included hijackings, hostage takings, kidnappings, car bombings, and, frequently, suicide bombings. Although apparently random, the victims and locations of terrorist attacks often are carefully selected for their shock value. Schools, shopping centres, bus and train stations, and restaurants and nightclubs have been targeted both because they attract large crowds and because they are places with which members of the civilian population are familiar and in which they feel at ease. The goal of terrorism generally is to destroy the public's sense of security in the places most familiar to them. Major targets sometimes also include buildings or other locations that are important economic or political symbols, such as embassies or military installations. The hope of the terrorist is that the sense of terror these acts engender will induce the population to pressure political leaders toward a specific political end.

Some definitions treat all acts of terrorism, regardless of their political motivations, as simple criminal activity. For example, in the United States the standard definition used by the Federal Bureau of Investigation (FBI) describes terrorism as "the unlawful use of force and violence against persons or property to intimidate or coerce a government, the civilian population, or any segment thereof, in furtherance of political or social objectives." The element of criminality, however, is problematic because it does not distinguish among different political and legal systems and thus cannot account for cases in which violent attacks against a government may be legitimate. A frequently mentioned example is the African National Congress (ANC) of South Africa, which committed violent actions against that country's apartheid government but commanded broad sympathy throughout the world. Another example is the Resistance movement against the Nazi occupation of France during World War II.

Since the 20th century, ideology and political opportunism have led a number of countries to engage in transnational terrorism, often under the guise of supporting movements of national liberation. (Hence, it became a common saying that "One man's terrorist is another man's freedom fighter.") The distinction between terrorism and other forms of political violence became blurred—particularly as many guerrilla groups often employed terrorist tactics—and issues of jurisdiction and legality were similarly obscured.

These problems have led some social scientists to adopt a definition of terrorism based not on criminality but on the fact that the victims of terrorist violence are most often innocent civilians. For example, the U.S. government eventually accepted the view that terrorism was premeditated, politically motivated violence perpetrated against noncombatant targets. Even this definition is flexible, however, and on occasion it has been expanded to include various other factors, such as that terrorist acts are clandestine or surreptitious, that terrorists choose their victims randomly, and that terrorist acts are intended to create an overwhelming sense of fear.

In the late 20th century, the term "ecoterrorism" was used to describe acts of environmental destruction committed in order to further a political goal or as an act of war, such as the burning of Kuwaiti oil wells by the Iraqi army during the Persian Gulf War. The term also was applied to certain environmentally benign though criminal acts, such as the spiking of lumber trees, intended to disrupt or prevent activities allegedly harmful to the environment.

## Types of Terrorism

Various attempts have been made to distinguish among types of terrorist activities. It is vital to bear in mind, however, that there are many kinds of terrorist movements, and no single theory can cover them all. Not only are the aims, members, beliefs, and resources of groups engaged in terrorism extremely diverse, but so are the political contexts of their campaigns. One popular typology identifies three broad classes of terrorism: revolutionary, subrevolutionary, and establishment terrorism. Although this typology has been

*Angelo Basone and Renato Curcio, members of the Red Brigades, in court in Milan, Italy, on Dec. 6, 1977.* Mondadori/Getty Images

criticized as inexhaustive, it provides a useful framework for understanding and evaluating terrorist activities.

Revolutionary terrorism is arguably the most common form. Practitioners of this type of terrorism seek the complete abolition of a political system and its replacement with new structures. Modern instances of such activity include campaigns by the Italian Red Brigades, the German Red Army Faction (Baader-Meinhof Gang), the Basque separatist group ETA, and the Peruvian Shining Path (Sendero Luminoso), each of which attempted to topple a national regime. Subrevolutionary terrorism is rather less common. It is used not to overthrow an existing regime but to modify the existing sociopolitical structure. Since this modification is often accomplished through the threat of deposing the existing regime, subrevolutionary groups are somewhat more difficult to identify. An example can be seen in the ANC and its campaign to end apartheid in South Africa.

Establishment terrorism, often called state or state-sponsored terrorism, is employed by governments—or more often by factions within governments—against that government's citizens, against factions within the government, or against foreign governments or groups. This type of terrorism is very common but difficult to identify, mainly because the state's support is always clandestine. The Soviet Union and its allies allegedly engaged in widespread support of international terrorism during the Cold War; in the 1980s the United States supported rebel groups in Africa that allegedly engaged in acts of terrorism, such as the National Union for the Total Independence of Angola (UNITA); and various Muslim countries (e.g., Iran and Syria) purportedly provided logistical and financial aid to Islamic revolutionary groups engaged in campaigns against Israel, the United States, and some Muslim countries in the late 20th and early 21st centuries.

The military dictatorships in Chile (1973–90) and Argentina (1976–83) committed acts of state terrorism against their own populations. The violent police states of Joseph Stalin in the Soviet Union and Ṣaddām Ḥussein in Iraq are examples of countries in which one organ of the government—often either the executive branch or the intelligence establishment—engaged in widespread terror against not only the population but also other organs of the government, including the military.

The persistent element of all forms of establishment terrorism, unlike that of nonstate terrorism, is that of secrecy. States invariably seek to disavow their active complicity in such acts, both to evade international censure and to avoid political and military retribution by those they target.

# The History of Terror

Terror has been practiced by state and nonstate actors throughout history and throughout the world. The ancient Greek historian Xenophon (c. 431–c. 350 BCE) wrote of the effectiveness of psychological warfare against enemy populations. Roman emperors such as Tiberius (reigned CE 14–37) and Caligula (reigned CE 37–41) used banishment, expropriation of property, and execution as means to discourage opposition to their rule.

The most commonly cited example of early terror, however, is the activity of the Jewish Zealots, often known as the Sicarii (Hebrew: "Daggers"), who engaged in frequent violent attacks on fellow Hebrews suspected of collusion with the Roman authorities. Likewise, the use of terror was openly advocated by Robespierre during the French Revolution, and the Spanish Inquisition used arbitrary arrest, torture, and execution to punish what it viewed as religious heresy. After the American Civil War (1861–65), defiant Southerners

*Adolf Hitler, circa 1930.* Roger Viollet/Getty Images

formed the Ku Klux Klan to intimidate supporters of Reconstruction (1865–77) and the newly freed former slaves. In the latter half of the 19th century, terror was adopted in western Europe, Russia, and the United States by adherents of anarchism, who believed that the best way to effect revolutionary political and social change was to assassinate persons in positions of power. From 1865 to 1905 a number of kings, presidents, prime ministers, and other government officials were killed by anarchists' guns or bombs.

The 20th century witnessed great changes in the use and practice of terror. It became the hallmark of a number of political movements stretching from the extreme right to the extreme left of the political spectrum. Technological advances, such as automatic weapons and compact, electrically detonated explosives, gave terrorists a new mobility and lethality, and the growth of air travel provided new methods and opportunities. Terrorism was virtually an official policy in totalitarian states such as those of Nazi Germany under Adolf Hitler and the Soviet Union under Stalin. In these states arrest, imprisonment, torture, and execution were carried out without legal guidance or restraints to create a climate of fear and to encourage adherence to the national ideology and the declared economic, social, and political goals of the state.

Terror has been used by one or both sides in anticolonial conflicts (e.g., Ireland and the United Kingdom, Algeria and France, and Vietnam and France and the United States), in disputes between different national groups over possession of a contested homeland (e.g., Palestinians and Israelis), in conflicts between different religious denominations (e.g., Catholics and Protestants in Northern Ireland), and in internal conflicts between revolutionary forces and established governments (e.g., in the successor states of the former Yugoslavia, Indonesia, the Philippines, Nicaragua, El Salvador, and Peru). In the late 20th and early 21st centuries some of the most extreme and destructive organizations that engaged in terrorism possessed a fundamentalist religious ideology (e.g., Ḥamās and al-Qaeda). Some groups, including the Liberation Tigers of Tamil Eelam and Ḥamās, adopted the tactic of suicide bombing, in which the perpetrator would attempt to destroy an important economic, military, political, or symbolic target by detonating a bomb on his person. In the latter half of the 20th century the most prominent groups using terrorist tactics were the Red Army Faction, the Japanese Red Army, the Red Brigades, the Puerto Rican FALN, Fatah and other groups related to the Palestine Liberation Organization (PLO), the Shining Path, and the Liberation Tigers.

In the late 20th century the United States suffered several acts of terrorist violence by Puerto Rican nationalists (such as the FALN), antiabortion groups, and foreign-based organizations. The 1990s witnessed some of the deadliest attacks on American soil, including the bombing of the World Trade Center in New York City in 1993 and the Oklahoma City bombing two years later, which killed 168 people. In addition, there were several major terrorist attacks on U.S. government targets overseas, including military bases in Saudi Arabia (1996) and the U.S. embassies in Kenya and Tanzania (1998). In 2000 an explosion triggered by suicide bombers caused the deaths of 17 sailors aboard a U.S. naval ship, the USS *Cole*, in the Yemeni port of Aden.

The deadliest terrorist strikes to date were the September 11 attacks (2001), in which suicide terrorists associated with al-Qaeda hijacked four commercial airplanes, crashing two of them into the twin towers of the World Trade Center complex in New York City and the third into the Pentagon building near Washington, D.C.; the fourth plane crashed near Pittsburgh, Pa. The crashes destroyed much of the World Trade Center complex and a large portion of one side of the Pentagon and killed more than 3,000 people.

Terrorism appears to be an enduring feature of political life. Even prior to the September 11 attacks, there was widespread concern that terrorists might escalate their destructive power to vastly greater proportions by using weapons of mass destruction—including nuclear, biological, or chemical weapons—as was done by the Japanese doomsday cult AUM Shinrikyo, which released nerve gas into a Tokyo subway in 1995. These fears were intensified after September 11, when a number of letters contaminated with anthrax were delivered to political leaders and journalists in the United States, leading to several deaths. U.S. Pres. George W. Bush made a broad war against terrorism the centrepiece of U.S. foreign policy at the beginning of the 21st century.

What follows is a look at some of the most notable terror groups, terrorist acts, and the people behind them.

# Fatah

Fatah is a political and military organization of Arab Palestinians founded in the late 1950s by Yāsir ʿArafāt and Khalīl al-Wazīr (Abū Jihād) with the aim of wresting Palestine from Israeli control by waging low-intensity guerrilla warfare.

Fatah obtained Syrian support and became based in Damascus. By 1963 Fatah had developed a commando-type organizational structure. In December 1964 it carried out its first military operation when it blew up an Israeli water-pump installation. By 1968 Fatah—then centred in Jordan—had emerged as a major Palestinian force and in March of that year was the primary target of an Israeli attack on the Jordanian village of Karameh in which 150 guerrillas and 29 Israelis were killed. The strong showing of Fatah at Karameh—especially after the Arab humiliation in the Six-Day War of 1967—boosted Fatah politically and psychologically. By the end of the 1960s it was the largest and best-funded of all the

*One of the eight Palestinian terrorists comprising the Black September group during a standoff after they kidnapped nine members of the Israeli Olympic team and killed two others, Sept. 5, 1972, in Munich, Germany.* Hulton Archive/Getty Images

Palestinian organizations and had taken over effective control of the Palestine Liberation Organization (PLO).

Following the civil war in Jordan (September 1970), the Jordanian army forced the PLO and Fatah fighters out of Jordan and into Lebanon, and in July 1971 Jordanian authorities killed a respected Fatah leader, Abū ʿAlī ʿIyād. An extremist militant corps of Fatah called Black September (Aylūl Aswad) subsequently emerged, first proclaimed in November 1971. It drew its first international notoriety in September 1972 when some of its members murdered 11 Israeli athletes at the Summer Olympic Games in Munich, West Germany. Black September was thereafter involved in a number of acts of terrorism, primarily against Israel.

In 1982 Israel's invasion of southern Lebanon, where Fatah had been headquartered, presented a further crisis. In an operation specifically intended to quiet Palestinian guerrilla activity along the Lebanese-Israeli border, the Israeli army ousted the PLO and Fatah from those areas of Lebanon not controlled by Syria; Tunis, Tunisia, became the next base of operations. Rival battling factions developed within Fatah during 1983, and a divisive leadership struggle developed. By the 1990s, however, ʿArafāt had reclaimed his leadership of Fatah, which remained the largest constituent member of the PLO.

In 1993 Israel and the Fatah-led PLO signed a peace agreement (the Oslo Accords) that was opposed by Ḥamās, a rival Islamic group. The following year the Palestinian Authority (PA) was established to govern the emerging Palestinian autonomous regions, and Gaza city became Fatah headquarters. Elections were held in PA-administered areas in 1996. ʿArafāt won the presidency, and Fatah captured a majority of seats within the Palestinian Legislative Council (PLC); Ḥamās did not participate in the elections. In 2005 Mahmoud Abbas, one of the original members of Fatah, was elected PA president, succeeding 'Arafāt, who had died the previous year.

In January 2006, elections were held for the PLC, and Fatah unexpectedly lost to Ḥamās, which won a majority of seats. Although the two groups eventually formed a tenuous coalition government, violence escalated between Ḥamās and Fatah forces in the Gaza Strip, leading Abbas to dissolve the Ḥamās-led government and declare a state of emergency in June 2007. Fatah thereafter exerted very little influence in the Gaza Strip, which was largely controlled by Ḥamās. Fatah's popularity was somewhat diminished, and it suffered from a reputation of inefficacy and corruption. However, Fatah—as the party leading the Palestinian governing body recognized by the international community—remained central to Israeli-Palestinian peace negotiations.

In August 2009 Fatah held its first congress in two decades. The meeting, held in the West Bank town of Bethlehem, was attended by some 2,000 delegates (the approximately 400 Fatah delegates in the Gaza Strip were not permitted by Ḥamās to attend).

In April 2011 Ḥamās and Fatah officials announced that the two sides had reached a reconciliation agreement in negotiations mediated by Egypt. The agreement, signed in Cairo on May 4, called for the formation of an interim government, to be followed in 2012 by legislative and presidential elections. After months of negotiations over the leadership of the interim government, the two parties announced in February 2012 that they had selected Abbas for the post of interim prime minister.

## Hamas

Hamas is the acronym of Ḥarakat al-Muqāwamah al-Islāmiyyah (English: Islamic Resistance Movement). Hamas

# Abū Niḍāl

Abū Niḍāl, byname of Ṣabrī Khalīl al-Bannā (1937–Aug. 16?, 2002), was a militant leader of the Fatah Revolutionary Council, more commonly known as the Abū Niḍāl Organization (ANO), or Abū Niḍāl Group, a Palestinian organization that engaged in numerous acts of terrorism beginning in the mid-1970s.

Abū Niḍāl and his family fled Palestine after the 1948 war following the creation of the state of Israel, and for the next 20 years he lived in Jordan and Saudi Arabia. In the late 1960s he joined Yāsir 'Arafāt's guerrilla group, Fatah, a component of the Palestine Liberation Organization (PLO), which had as its aim wresting Palestine from Israeli control. He left the group in 1973 because of his dissatisfaction with moderates within Fatah who were willing to pursue diplomatic solutions to the Palestinian question. His new organization, no longer associated with Fatah, operated out of Iraq, then Syria, and finally Libya, usually with the support of those governments. Many of his targets were fellow Palestinians whose political views were at odds with his own, and at a 1974 tribunal the PLO condemned Abū Niḍāl as an extremist, sentencing him to death in absentia.

The ANO was held responsible for terrorist attacks against both Arab and Israeli diplomats and government representatives in the Middle East and Europe. It also was alleged to have carried out hijackings (including that of an Egyptian airliner that resulted in the deaths of 60 people in 1985), bombings, and commando raids. Among its most infamous acts were the simultaneous attacks at the international airports in Rome and Vienna in December 1985, in which 18 people were killed, and the shooting of 21 worshipers in an Istanbul synagogue in 1986. In January 1991 Abū Niḍāl's agents were thought to have been responsible for the assassination of Abū 'Iyād (nom de guerre of Ṣalāḥ Khalaf), the PLO's intelligence chief and one of 'Arafāt's closest associates. In 2001 Abū Niḍāl was condemned to death, again in absentia, by a court in Jordan for the 1994 murder of a

Jordanian diplomat. At the height of its activity, the ANO never enjoyed broad popular support among the Palestinian people, and its active members never exceeded a few hundred. Although it was among the world's most violent organizations engaging in terrorism in the 1970s and '80s, the group's activities diminished in the 1990s.

Expelled from numerous countries and pursued by his enemies, Abū Niḍāl was forced to move frequently, eventually settling in Baghdad, Iraq. He died there in 2002 while in the custody of Iraqi authorities.

is a militant Palestinian Islamic movement in the West Bank and Gaza Strip that is dedicated to the destruction of Israel and the creation of an Islamic state in Palestine. Founded in 1987, Ḥamās opposed the 1993 peace accords between Israel and the PLO.

From the late 1970s, Islamic activists connected with the pan-Islamic Muslim Brotherhood established a network of charities, clinics, and schools and became active in the territories (the Gaza Strip and West Bank) occupied by Israel after the 1967 Six-Day War. In Gaza they were active in many mosques, while their activities in the West Bank generally were limited to the universities. The Muslim Brotherhood's activities in these areas were generally nonviolent, but a number of small groups in the occupied territories began to call for jihad, or holy war, against Israel. In December 1987, at the beginning of the Palestinian intifada (from Arabic *intifāḍ ah*, "shaking off") movement against Israeli occupation, Ḥamās (which also is an Arabic word meaning "zeal") was established by members of the Muslim Brotherhood and religious factions of the PLO, and the new organization quickly acquired a broad following. In its 1988 charter, Ḥamās maintained that Palestine is an Islamic homeland that can never be surrendered to non-Muslims and that waging holy war to wrest control of Palestine from Israel is a religious duty for Palestinian Muslims. This position brought it into conflict with the PLO, which in 1988 recognized Israel's right to exist.

Ḥamās soon began to act independently of other Palestinian organizations, generating animosity between the group and its secular nationalist counterparts. Increasingly violent Ḥamās attacks on civilian and military targets impelled Israel to arrest a number of Ḥamās leaders in 1989, including Sheikh Ahmed Yassin, the movement's founder. In the years that followed, Ḥamās underwent reorganization to reinforce its command structure and locate key leaders out of Israel's reach. A political bureau responsible for the organization's international relations and fund-raising was formed in Amman, Jordan, and the group's armed wing was reconstituted as the 'Izz al-Dīn al-Qassām Forces.

*Masked militants of 'Izz al-Dīn al-Qassām Forces, in Rafah, southern Gaza Strip, on Nov. 14, 2013.* Said Khatib/AFP/Getty Images

Ḥamās denounced the 1993 peace agreement between Israel and the PLO and, along with the Islamic Jihad group, subsequently intensified its terror campaign using suicide bombers. The PLO and Israel responded with harsh security and punitive measures, although PLO chairman Yāsir ʿArafāt, seeking to include Ḥamās in the political process, appointed Ḥamās members to leadership positions in the Palestinian Authority (PA). The collapse of peace talks between Israelis and Palestinians in September 2000 led to an increase in violence that came to be known as the Aqṣā intifada. That conflict was marked by a degree of violence unseen in the first intifada, and Ḥamās activists further escalated their attacks on Israelis and engaged in a number of suicide bombings in Israel itself. Jordan expelled Ḥamās leaders from Amman in 1999, accusing them of having used their Jordanian offices as a command post for military activities in the West Bank and Gaza. In 2001 the political bureau established new headquarters in Damascus, Syria.

In early 2005 Mahmoud Abbas, president of the PA, and Israeli Prime Minister Ariel Sharon announced a suspension of hostilities as Israel prepared to withdraw troops from some Palestinian territories. After much negotiation, Ḥamās agreed to the cease-fire, although sporadic violence continued. In the 2006 elections for the Palestinian Legislative Council, Ḥamās won a surprise victory over Fatah, capturing the majority of seats. The two groups eventually formed a coalition government, though clashes between Ḥamās and Fatah forces in the Gaza Strip intensified, prompting Abbas to dissolve the Ḥamās-led government and declare a state of emergency in June 2007. Ḥamās was left in control of the Gaza Strip, while a Fatah-led emergency cabinet had control of the West Bank.

Later that year Israel declared the Gaza Strip under Ḥamās a hostile entity and approved a series of sanctions that included power cuts, heavily restricted imports, and border closures. Ḥamās attacks on Israel continued, as did Israeli attacks on the Gaza Strip. After months of negotiations, in June 2008 Israel and Ḥamās agreed to implement a truce scheduled to last six months; however, this was threatened shortly thereafter as each accused the other of violations, which escalated in the last months of the agreement. On December 19 the truce officially expired amid accusations of violations on both sides. Broader hostilities erupted shortly thereafter as Israel, responding to sustained rocket fire, mounted a series of air strikes across the region—among the strongest in years—meant to target Ḥamās. After a week of air strikes, Israeli forces initiated a ground campaign into the Gaza Strip amid calls from the international community for a cease-fire. Following more than three weeks of hostilities—in which perhaps more than 1,000 were killed and tens of thousands left homeless—Israel and Ḥamās each declared a unilateral cease-fire.

In April 2011 Ḥamās and Fatah officials announced that the two sides had reached a reconciliation agreement in negotiations mediated by Egypt. The agreement, signed in Cairo on May 4, called for the formation of an interim government to organize legislative and presidential elections in 2012. After months of negotiations over the leadership of the interim government, the two parties announced in February 2012 that they had selected Abbas for the post of interim prime minister.

Ḥamās's relations with the governments of Syria and Iran, two of its primary sources of support, were strained in 2011 when Ḥamās leaders in Damascus conspicuously avoided expressing support for a crackdown by Syrian armed forces against antigovernment protesters inside the country. In early 2012 Ḥamās leaders left Syria for Egypt and Qatar and then publicly declared their support for the Syrian opposition.

Beginning on Nov. 14, 2012, Israel launched a series of air strikes in Gaza, in response to an increase in the number of rockets fired from Gaza into Israeli territory over the previous nine months. The head of the 'Izz al-Dīn al-Qassām Forces, Ahmed Said Khalil al-Jabari, was killed in the initial strike. Ḥamās retaliated with increasing rocket attacks on Israel, and hostilities continued until Israel and Ḥamās reached a cease-fire agreement on November 21.

# Democratic Front for the Liberation of Palestine (DFLP)

One of several organizations associated with the PLO, the Democratic Front for the Liberation of Palestine (DFLP) engaged in acts of terrorism in the 1970s and '80s and originally maintained a Marxist-Leninist orientation, believing the peasants and the working classes should be educated in socialism in order to bring about a democratic state of Jews and Arabs free of Zionism and imperialism.

Originating in the leftist swing of the 1960s and founded by a Jordanian Orthodox Christian, Nayif Hawātmeh, in 1969, the Popular Democratic Front for the Liberation of Palestine (as it was originally named) was envisioned as a political movement distinct from the Popular Front for the Liberation of Palestine (PFLP), which had been founded to provide an umbrella group for militant Palestinian groups. The DFLP stood ideologically to the left of the PFLP and claimed that its enemies were Zionist upper-class colonists. In 1974 it took responsibility for an especially brutal terrorist attack in Ma'alot, Israel, in which several dozen schoolchildren were taken hostage and a number of them killed, and another raid in Bet She'an. The DFLP was wary of becoming too closely associated with Arab governments and was critical of other pro-Palestine groups for ignoring conservative forces within the Arab world. Its leaders were among the earliest proponents of a Palestinian "national authority," which eventually evolved into a call for a Palestinian state alongside Israel. The PLO adopted this proposal in 1974.

# Popular Front for the Liberation of Palestine (PFLP)

The Popular Front for the Liberation of Palestine (PFLP) is an organization providing an institutional framework for militant organizations associated with the PLO, notable for its Marxist-Leninist ideology and its hijacking of a number of aircraft between 1968 and 1974.

The PFLP was established in 1967 in an amalgamation of three different guerrilla groups by the militant Palestinian leader George Ḥabash. Conflicts within the organization over ideology led to several splits and generated independent factions, most notably the PFLP-General Command (PFLP-GC) established in 1968 by Aḥmad Jibrīl. Each of these factions engaged in guerrilla activity against Israel and often undertook acts of terrorism against the Jewish state and Western interests. The PFLP itself carried out or organized many notorious attacks against Israeli and Western targets, most notably the hijacking and destruction of several commercial airliners in the late 1960s and early '70s. The PFLP rejected political compromise with Israel—it opposed the peace process begun with Israel in the 1990s—and pledged to replace that state with a secular, democratic state in Palestine. It took a vigorously anti-Western and anticapitalist stance on other Middle Eastern questions. Ḥabash retired as head of the organization in 2000; his successor, Abū 'Alī Muṣṭafā, was killed by Israeli forces in the PFLP's West Bank offices in 2001.

# George Ḥabash

George Ḥabash (1925/26–Jan. 26, 2008) was a militant Palestinian and leader of the Popular Front for the Liberation of Palestine (PFLP).

Ḥabash was forced to flee Palestine in 1948, after the State of Israel was established there, and earned a medical degree at the American University of Beirut. In the early 1950s he was active in the "Youth of Vengeance" group, which advocated violent attacks on traditional Arab governments. Ḥabash founded the militant PFLP after his goal to liberate Palestine through Arab unity proved unrealistic following the Arab defeat by Israel in the Six-Day War of 1967. Under the leadership of Ḥabash, the PFLP staged several airplane hijackings, including the abduction of three Western passenger jets to a Jordanian airstrip in September 1970. These activities destabilized the Jordanian monarchy and triggered King Ḥussein's crackdown on Palestinian guerrillas operating in Jordan. A bloody civil war followed, in which the PFLP and other guerrillas were driven from the country.

Ḥabash, a Marxist, visited China in 1970 (where Chinese leaders criticized the PFLP's "foreign operations") and Moscow in 1972. Following the Yom Kippur War of 1973, Ḥabash became the leading voice of the "Rejection Front," four Palestinian groups that opposed any diplomatic settlement to the conflict with Israel. He attacked what he called the "defeatist" attitude of the Palestine Liberation Organization's leadership, whose attempts at reconciliation with King Ḥussein he sharply criticized. Under his leadership the PFLP successfully organized clandestine cells in the Israeli-occupied West Bank and Gaza Strip. Ḥabash stepped down as leader of the PLFP in 2000.

# Palestine Liberation Organization (PLO)

The Palestine Liberation Organization (PLO) is a political organization claiming to represent the world's Palestinians—those Arabs, and their descendants, who lived in mandated Palestine before the creation there of the State of Israel in 1948. It was formed in 1964 to centralize the leadership of various Palestinian groups that previously had operated as clandestine resistance movements. It came into prominence only after the Six-Day War of June 1967, however, and engaged in a protracted guerrilla war against Israel during the 1960s, '70s, and '80s before entering into peace negotiations with that country in the 1990s.

## Foundation and Early Development

After the Arab-Israeli war of 1948 the Arab states, notably Egypt, took the lead in the political and military struggle against Israel. The Palestinians themselves had been dispersed among a number of countries, and—lacking an organized central leadership—many Palestinians formed small, diffuse resistance organizations, often under the patronage of the various Arab states; as a result, Palestinian political activity was limited.

The PLO was created at an Arab summit meeting in 1964 in order to bring various Palestinian groups together under one organization, but at first it did little to enhance Palestinian self-determination. The PLO's legislature, the Palestine National Council (PNC), was composed of members from the civilian population of various Palestinian communities, and its charter (the Palestine National Charter, or Covenant) set out the goals of the organization, which included the complete elimination of Israeli sovereignty in Palestine and the destruction of the State of Israel. Yet, the PLO's first chairman, a former diplomat named Aḥmad Shuqayrī, was closely tied to Egypt, its military force (the Palestine Liberation Army, formed in 1968) was integrated into the armies of surrounding Arab states, and the militant guerrilla organizations under its auspices had only limited influence on PLO policy. Likewise, although the PLO received its funding from taxes levied on the salaries of Palestinian workers, for decades the organization also depended heavily on the contributions of sympathetic countries.

## Expansion and the Rise of Yāsir ʿArafāt

It was only after the defeat of the Arab states by Israel in the Six-Day War of June 1967 that the PLO began to be widely recognized as the representative of the Palestinians and came to promote a distinctively Palestinian agenda. The defeat discredited the Arab states, and Palestinians sought greater autonomy in their struggle with Israel. In 1968 leaders of Palestinian guerrilla factions gained representation in the PNC, and the influence of the more militant and independent-minded groups within the PLO increased. Major PLO factions or those associated with it included Fatah (since 1968 the preeminent faction within the PLO), the Popular Front for the Liberation of Palestine (PFLP), the Democratic Front for the Liberation of Palestine (DFLP), and al-Ṣāʿiqah. Over the decades the PLO's membership has varied as its constituent bodies have reorganized and disagreed internally. The more radical factions have remained steadfast in their goals of the destruction of Israel and its replacement with a secular state in which Muslims, Jews, and Christians would, ostensibly, participate as equals. Moderate factions within the PLO, however, have proved willing to accept a negotiated settlement with Israel that would yield a Palestinian state, which at times has led to internecine violence.

In 1969 Yāsir 'Arafāt, leader of Fatah, was named the PLO's chairman. From the late 1960s the PLO organized and launched guerrilla attacks against Israel from its bases in Jordan, which prompted significant Israeli reprisals and led to instability within Jordan. This, in turn, brought the PLO into growing conflict with the government of King Ḥussein of Jordan in 1970, and in 1971 the PLO was forcibly expelled from the country by the Jordanian army. Thereafter the PLO shifted its bases to Lebanon and continued its attacks on Israel. The PLO's relations with the Lebanese were tumultuous, and the organization soon became embroiled in Lebanon's sectarian disputes and contributed to that country's eventual slide into civil war. During that time, factions within the PLO shifted from attacks on military targets to a strategy of terrorism—a policy the organization fervently denied embracing—and a number of high-profile attacks, including bombings and aircraft hijackings, were staged by PLO operatives against Israeli and Western targets.

From 1974 'Arafāt advocated an end to the PLO's attacks on targets outside of Israel and sought the world community's acceptance of the PLO as the legitimate representative of the Palestinian people. In 1974 the Arab heads of state recognized the PLO as the sole legitimate representative of all Palestinians, and the PLO was admitted to full membership in the Arab League in 1976. Yet the PLO was excluded from the negotiations between Egypt and Israel that resulted in 1979 in a peace treaty that returned the Israeli-occupied Sinai Peninsula to Egypt but failed to win Israel's agreement to the establishment of a Palestinian state in the occupied territories of the West Bank and Gaza Strip.

Israel's desire to destroy the PLO and its bases in Lebanon led Israel to invade that country in June 1982. Israeli troops soon surrounded the Lebanese capital of Beirut, which for several years had been the PLO's headquarters. Following negotiations, PLO forces evacuated Beirut and were transported to sympathetic Arab countries.

Increasing dissatisfaction with 'Arafāt's leadership arose in the PLO after he withdrew from Beirut to Tunis, Tunisia, and in 1983 Syrian-backed PLO rebels supported by Syrian troops forced 'Arafāt's remaining troops out of Lebanon. 'Arafāt retained the support of some Arab leaders and eventually was able to reassert his leadership of the PLO.

## Two Intifadas and the Search for Peace

Bereft of bases from which PLO forces might attack the Jewish state and encouraged by the success of a popular uprising, the intifada (Arabic: "shaking off"), that began in 1987 in the occupied territories, the PLO leadership developed a more flexible and conciliatory policy toward peace with Israel. On Nov. 15, 1988, the PLO proclaimed the "State of Palestine," a kind of government-in-exile; and on April 2, 1989, the PNC elected 'Arafāt president of the new quasi-state. The PLO during this period also recognized United Nations Resolutions 242 and 338, thereby tacitly acknowledging Israel's right to exist. It thus abandoned its long-standing goal of replacing Israel with a secular, democratic state in Palestine in favour of a policy accepting separate Israeli and Palestinian states, with the latter occupying the West Bank and the Gaza Strip.

'Arafāt's decision to support Iraq during the 1990–91 Persian Gulf War alienated the PLO's key financial donors among the gulf oil states and contributed to a further softening of its position regarding peace with Israel. In April 1993 the PLO under 'Arafāt's leadership entered secret negotiations with Israel on a possible peace settlement between the two sides. The first document in a set of Israel-PLO agreements— generally termed the Oslo Accords—was signed on Sept. 13, 1993, by 'Arafāt and the leaders of the Israeli government. The

# Khalīl Ibrāhām al-Wazīr

Khalīl Ibrāhīm al-Wazīr (Oct. 10, 1935–April 16, 1988) was a Palestinian leader who became the mil-itary strategist and second in command of the Palestine Liberation Organization (PLO).

Wazīr fled from Ramla with his family during the 1948 war that followed the creation of the State of Israel. He grew up in the Gaza Strip, where he was educated by the United Nations Relief and Works Agency. He met future PLO leader Yāsir 'Arafāt in 1951 while attending college in Cairo, and together they organized anti-Israel guerrilla actions and founded the militant organization Fatah (1958), which merged with smaller groups to form the PLO (1964). As 'Arafāt's deputy and a moderate within the PLO, Wazīr often negotiated with PLO extremists, maintained diplomatic relations with other countries, and reportedly planned military strategies and arranged arms purchases for Fatah and the PLO. After the PLO was expelled from Jordan in 1971, he eventually became an advocate of rapprochement with Jordan and played a role in increasing the PLO's emphasis on work in the West Bank and Gaza Strip. These efforts contributed to a general Palestinian uprising known as the intifada in 1987. He was killed in his home in Tunis by Israeli commandos.

agreements called for mutual recognition between the two sides and set out conditions under which the West Bank and Gaza would be gradually handed over to the newly formed Palestinian Authority, of which 'Arafāt was to become the first president. This transfer was originally to have taken place over a five-year interim period in which Israel and the Palestinians were to have negotiated a permanent settlement. Despite some success, however, negotiations faltered sporadically throughout the 1990s and collapsed completely amid increasing violence— dubbed the Aqṣā intifada—in late 2000. This second uprising had a distinctly religious character, and militant Islamic groups such as Ḥamās, which had come to the fore during the first intifada, attracted an ever-larger following and threatened the PLO's dominance within Palestinian society.

# Irgun Zvai Leumi

Irgun Zvai Leumi was a Jewish right-wing underground movement in Palestine, founded in 1931. At first supported by many nonsocialist Zionist parties, in opposition to the Haganah, it became in 1936 an instrument of the Revisionist Party, an extreme nationalist group that had seceded from the World Zionist Organization and whose policies called for the use of force, if necessary, to establish a Jewish state on both sides of the Jordan.

Irgun committed acts of terrorism and assassination against the British, whom it regarded as illegal occupiers, and it was also violently anti-Arab. Irgun participated in the organization of illegal immigration into Palestine after the publication of the British White Paper on Palestine (1939), which severely limited immigration. Irgun's violent activities led to execution of many of its members by the British; in retaliation, Irgun executed British army hostages.

Irgun's members were extremely disciplined and daring, and their actions included the capture of 'Akko (Acre) prison, a medieval fortress that not even Napoleon had succeeded in capturing. In the last days of the British mandate, it captured a large part of the city of Yafo (Jaffa).

On July 22, 1946, Irgun blew up a wing of the King David Hotel in Jerusalem, killing 91 soldiers and civilians (British, Arab, and Jewish). On April 9, 1947, a group of Irgun commandos raided the Arab village of Dayr Yāsīn (modern Kefar Sha'ul), killing about 100 of its inhabitants.

After the creation of Israel in 1948 Irgun's last units disbanded and took the oath of loyalty to the Israel Defense

Forces on Sept. 1, 1948. Politically, it was the precursor of the Ḥerut (Freedom) Party, one of Israel's most militant right-wing groups, which later merged with the Liberals into the Gaḥal Party.

# Hezbollah

Hezbollah, also spelled Hezbullah or Hizbullah, is a militia group and political party that first emerged as a faction in Lebanon following the Israeli invasion of that country in 1982.

Shī'ite Muslims, traditionally the weakest religious group in Lebanon, first found their voice in the moderate and largely secular Amal movement. Following the Islamic Revolution in Shī'ite Iran in 1979 and the Israeli invasion of Lebanon in 1982, a group of Lebanese Shī'ite clerics formed Hezbollah with the goal of driving Israel from Lebanon and establishing an Islamic state there. Hezbollah was based in the predominately Shī'ite areas of the Biqā' Valley, southern Lebanon, and southern Beirut. It coordinated its efforts closely with Iran, from which it acquired substantial logistical support, and drew its manpower largely from disaffected younger, more radical members of Amal. Throughout the 1980s Hezbollah engaged in increasingly sophisticated attacks against Israel and fought in Lebanon's civil war (1975–90), repeatedly coming to blows with Amal. During that time, Hezbollah allegedly engaged in terrorist attacks including kidnappings and car bombings, directed predominantly against Westerners, but also established a comprehensive social services network for its supporters.

Hezbollah was one of the few militia groups not disarmed by the Syrians at the end of the civil war, and they continued to fight a sustained guerrilla campaign against Israel in southern Lebanon until Israel's withdrawal in 2000.

Hezbollah emerged as a leading political party in post-civil war Lebanon.

On July 12, 2006, Hezbollah, in an attempt to pressure Israel into releasing three Lebanese jailed in Israeli prisons, launched a military operation against Israel, killing a number of Israeli soldiers and abducting two as prisoners of war. This action led Israel to launch a major military offensive against Hezbollah. The 34-day war between Hezbollah and Israel resulted in the deaths of more than 1,000 Lebanese and the displacement of some 1,000,000. Fighting the Israeli Defense Forces to a standstill—a feat no other Arab militia had accomplished—Hezbollah and its leader, Hassan Nasrallah, emerged as heroes throughout much of the Arab world. In the months following the war, Hezbollah used its prestige to attempt to topple Lebanon's government after its demands for more cabinet seats were not met: its members, along with those of the Amal militia, resigned from the cabinet. The opposition then declared that the remaining cabinet had lost its legitimacy and demanded the formation of a new government in which Hezbollah and its opposition allies would possess the power of veto.

Late the following year, efforts by the National Assembly to select a successor at the end of Lebanese Pres. Émile Lahoud's nine-year term were stalemated by the continued power struggle between the Hezbollah-led opposition and the Western-backed government. A boycott by the opposition—which continued to seek the veto power it had been denied—prevented the assembly from reaching a two-thirds quorum. Lahoud's term expired in November 2007, and the presidency remained unoccupied as the factions struggled to reach a consensus on a candidate and the makeup of the new government.

In May 2008, clashes between Hezbollah forces and government supporters in Beirut were sparked by government

*Members of the Lebanese Shīʿite Hezbollah movement carry the coffin of Ali Bazzi in a Shīʿite district of the Lebanese southern port of Sidon (Saida) on Dec. 9, 2013.* Mahmoud Zayyat/AFP/Getty Images

decisions that included plans to dismantle Hezbollah's private telecommunications network. Nasrallah equated the government decisions with a declaration of war and mobilized Hezbollah forces, which quickly took control of parts of Beirut. In the following days the government reversed the decisions that had sparked the outbreak of violence, and a summit attended by both factions in Qatar led to an agreement granting the Hezbollah-led opposition the veto power it had long sought.

In July 2008 Hezbollah and Israel concluded an agreement securing the exchange of several Lebanese prisoners and the remains of Lebanese and Palestinian fighters in return for the remains of Israeli soldiers, including the bodies of two soldiers whose capture by Hezbollah had sparked the brief war two years earlier.

In November 2009, after months of negotiations following National Assembly elections, Hezbollah and its allies agreed to form a unity government with Prime Minister Saad al-Hariri's March 14 bloc. Tension arose in 2010, following reports that the UN Special Tribunal for Lebanon, investigating the assassination of former Prime Minister Rafiq al-Hariri, had focused its investigation on senior Hezbollah officials and that it would soon issue indictments. Nasrallah condemned the tribunal as politically biased and compromised by forged evidence, and he called for the Lebanese government to stop cooperating with the investigation. The March 14 bloc continued to support the tribunal, resulting in a tense standoff. After attempts by Syria and Saudi Arabia to mediate between the two sides failed, Hezbollah forced the collapse of the unity government by withdrawing its two ministers and nine allied ministers from the cabinet. In January 2011 Najib Mikati, a Sunni billionaire, was nominated to be prime minister after receiving the backing of Hezbollah and its allies in parliament. Mikati's appointment, a sign of Hezbollah's increasing political strength, triggered protests by supporters of the March 14 bloc, who charged that the new government would be too closely aligned with Iran and Syria, Hezbollah's principle supporters. In June 2011, after five months of deliberations, Mikati announced the formation of a new 30-member cabinet, with 18 of the posts filled by Hezbollah allies. No posts were assigned to members of the March 14 bloc.

In late June 2011 the UN Special Tribunal for Lebanon issued arrest warrants for four suspects in the killing of Rafiq al-Hariri, who were identified by Lebanese officials as Hezbollah commanders and operatives. In response, Nasrallah denounced the tribunal and vowed never to turn over the four suspects.

# 'Abbās al-Mūsawī

'Abbās al-Mūsawī (*c.* 1952–February 16, 1992) was a Lebanese Shī'ite Muslim cleric and secretary-general (1991–92) of the militant Hezbollah ("Party of God") movement.

Mūsawī studied at a Shī'ite *madrasah* (religious college) in Al-Najaf, Iraq, where he was strongly influenced by the teachings of Iranian cleric Ayatollah Ruhollah Khomeini. Mūsawī returned to Lebanon in 1978 and four years later—inspired by the successful Khomeini-led Islamic revolution in Iran—helped to form Hezbollah in an effort to resist the Israeli occupation of southern Lebanon (1982) and to promote Shī'ite interests in that country. Although he denied any direct involvement in acts of terrorism, many Western observers believed that under his leadership Hezbollah was responsible for a number of terrorist actions, including the 1983 bombing attacks in Beirut that killed some 300 U.S. and French peace-keeping troops. After he was named secretary-general of Hezbollah, Mūsawī publicly denounced such attacks and endorsed more moderate policies. He was killed by an Israeli helicopter strike on his motorcade.

A wave of popular uprisings in early 2011, known as the Arab Spring, left Hezbollah in a difficult position. After applauding revolutionary movements in Tunisia, Egypt, Libya, and Bahrain, the group found its interests threatened by a similar movement against a key ally, Syrian Pres. Bashar al-Assad. As protests spread throughout Syria and the civilian death toll mounted, Nasrallah spoke out in support of Assad, echoing Assad's denunciations of the Syrian opposition as being agents of a foreign conspiracy. The conflict soon escalated into a full-blown civil war, and by late 2012 it was widely reported that Hezbollah fighters had been covertly sent to Syria to fight alongside the Syrian army. In May 2013,

Nasrallah publicly confirmed Hezbollah's involvement and vowed to fight until the rebels had been defeated.

# Al-Qaeda

Al-Qaeda is a broad-based militant Islamist organization founded by Osama bin Laden in the late 1980s.

Al-Qaeda began as a logistical network to support Muslims fighting against the Soviet Union during the Afghan War; members were recruited throughout the Islamic world. When the Soviets withdrew from Afghanistan in 1989, the organization dispersed but continued to oppose what its leaders considered corrupt Islamic regimes and foreign (i.e., U.S.) presence in Islamic lands. Based in Sudan for a period in the early 1990s, the group eventually reestablished its headquarters in Afghanistan (*c.* 1996) under the patronage of the Taliban militia.

Al-Qaeda merged with a number of other militant Islamist organizations, including Egypt's Islamic Jihad and the Islamic Group, and on several occasions its leaders declared holy war against the United States. The organization established camps for Muslim militants from throughout the world, training tens of thousands in paramilitary skills, and its agents engaged in numerous terrorist attacks, including the destruction of the U.S. embassies in Nairobi, Kenya, and Dar es Salaam, Tanzania (1998), and a suicide bomb attack against the U.S. warship *Cole* in Aden, Yemen (2000). In 2001, 19 militants associated with al-Qaeda staged the September 11 attacks against the United States. Within weeks the U.S. government responded by attacking Taliban and al-Qaeda forces in Afghanistan. Thousands of militants were killed or captured, among them several key members (including the militant who allegedly planned and organized the September 11 attacks), and the remainder and their leaders were driven into hiding.

*Osama bin Laden.* CNN/Getty Images

The invasion of Afghanistan in 2001 challenged that country's viability as an al-Qaeda sanctuary and training ground and compromised communication, operational, and financial linkages between al-Qaeda leadership and its militants. Rather than significantly weakening al-Qaeda, however, these realities prompted a structural evolution and the growth of "franchising." Increasingly, attacks were orchestrated not only from above by the centralized leadership (after the U.S. invasion of Afghanistan, based in the Afghan-Pakistani border regions) but also by the localized, relatively autonomous cells it encouraged. Such grassroots independent groups—coalesced locally around a common agenda but subscribing to the al-Qaeda name and its broader ideology—thus meant a diffuse form of militancy, and one far more difficult to confront.

With this organizational shift, al-Qaeda was linked—whether directly or indirectly—to more attacks in the six years following September 11 than it had been in the six years prior, including attacks in Jordan, Kenya, Saudi Arabia, Indonesia, Turkey, the United Kingdom, Israel, Algeria, and elsewhere. At the same time, al-Qaeda increasingly utilized the Internet as an expansive venue for communication and recruitment and as a mouthpiece for video messages, broadcasts, and propaganda. Meanwhile, some observers expressed concern that U.S. strategy—centred primarily on attempts to overwhelm al-Qaeda militarily—was ineffectual, and at the end of the first decade of the 21st century, al-Qaeda was thought to have reached its greatest strength since the attacks of September 2001.

On May 2, 2011, bin Laden was killed by U.S. military forces after U.S. intelligence located him residing in a secure compound in Abbottabad, Pakistan, 31 miles (50 km) from Islamabad. The operation was carried out by a small team that reached the compound in Abbottabad by helicopter. After bin Laden's death was confirmed, it was announced by U.S. Pres. Barack Obama, who hailed the operation as a major success in the fight against al-Qaeda. On June 16, 2011, al-Qaeda released a statement announcing that Ayman al-Zawahiri, bin Laden's long-serving deputy, had been appointed to replace bin Laden as the organization's leader.

## Osama bin Laden

Osama bin Laden, also spelled Usāmah ibn Lādin (1957–May 2, 2011) was the founder of the militant Islamist organization al-Qaeda and mastermind of numerous terrorist attacks against the United States and other Western powers, including the 2000 suicide bombing of the U.S. warship *Cole* in the Yemeni port of Aden and the Sept. 11, 2001, attacks on the

World Trade Center in New York City and the Pentagon near Washington, D.C.

Bin Laden was one of more than 50 children of Muhammad bin Laden, a self-made billionaire who, after emigrating to Saudi Arabia from Yemen as a labourer, rose to direct major construction projects for the Saudi royal family. By the time of Muhammad's death in an airplane accident in 1967, his company had become one of the largest construction firms in the Middle East, and the bin Laden family had developed a close relationship with the Saudi royal family.

Osama bin Laden studied business administration at King Abdul Aziz University in Jiddah, where it is likely that he also received instruction in religious studies from Muḥammad Quṭb, brother of the Islamic revivalist Sayyid Quṭb, and Abdullah Azzam, a militant leader. Shortly after the Soviet Union invaded Afghanistan in 1979, bin Laden, who viewed the invasion as an act of aggression against Islam, began traveling to meet Afghan resistance leaders and raise funds for the resistance. By 1984 his activities were centred mainly in Afghanistan and Pakistan, where he collaborated with Azzam to recruit and organize Arab volunteers to fight the Soviet occupation. Bin Laden's financial resources, along with his reputation for piety and for bravery in combat, enhanced his stature as a militant leader. A computer database he created in 1988 listing the names of volunteers for the Afghan War led to the formation that year of a new militant network named al-Qaeda (Arabic: "the Base"), although the group remained without clear objectives or an operational agenda for several years.

In 1989, following the Soviet withdrawal from Afghanistan, bin Laden returned to Saudi Arabia, where he was initially welcomed as a hero, but he soon came to be regarded by the government as a radical and a potential threat. In 1990 the government denied his requests for permission to use his network of fighters to defend Saudi Arabia against the threat of invasion posed by Ṣaddām Ḥussein's Iraq. Bin Laden was outraged when Saudi Arabia relied instead on U.S. troops for protection during the Persian Gulf War, leading to a growing rift between bin Laden and the country's leaders, and in 1991 he left Saudi Arabia, settling in Sudan at the end of the year.

In the early 1990s bin Laden and his al-Qaeda network began to formulate an agenda of violent struggle against the threat of U.S. dominance in the Muslim world. Bin Laden publicly praised other groups' attacks on Americans, including the 1993 bombing of the World Trade Center in New York. In 1994, as bin Laden expanded his group's infrastructure in Sudan and trained Islamic militants to participate in conflicts around the world, Saudi Arabia revoked his citizenship and froze his assets, forcing him to rely on outside sources for funding.

In 1996, under heavy international pressure, Sudan expelled bin Laden, and he returned to Afghanistan, where he received protection from its ruling Taliban militia. Later that year bin Laden issued the first of two *fatwās* (Arabic: "religious opinions") declaring a holy war against the United States, which he accused, among other things, of looting the natural resources of the Muslim world, occupying the Arabian Peninsula, including the holy sites of Islam, and supporting governments servile to U.S. interests in the Middle East. Bin Laden's apparent goal was to draw the United States into a large-scale war in the Muslim world that would overthrow moderate Muslim governments and reestablish the Caliphate (i.e., a single Islamic state).

To this end, al-Qaeda trained militants and funded terrorist attacks. In 1998 bin Laden ordered an operation larger than any of al-Qaeda's previous operations—simultaneous bombings of U.S. embassies in Nairobi, Kenya, and Dar es Salaam, Tanzania, which altogether killed 224 people. The

United States retaliated by launching cruise missiles at sites believed to be bin Laden's bases in Afghanistan. Another al-Qaeda bombing in 2000 targeted the USS *Cole*, an American warship harboured in Yemen, and killed 17 sailors.

At the end of the 20th century, bin Laden was thought to have had thousands of militant followers worldwide, in places as diverse as Saudi Arabia, Yemen, Libya, Bosnia, Chechnya, and the Philippines. In 2001, after 19 militants associated with al-Qaeda staged the September 11 attacks, the United States led a coalition that overthrew the Taliban in Afghanistan. In December 2001 bin Laden went into hiding after evading capture by U.S. forces in the Tora Bora cave complex. In the following years U.S. forces searched for him along the Afghanistan-Pakistan border, during which time bin Laden remained absent from the public eye. Then in October 2004—less than a week before that year's U.S. presidential election—bin Laden emerged in a videotaped message in which he claimed responsibility for the September 11 attacks. After that he periodically released audio messages, including in 2008, when he threatened retaliation for the deaths of Palestinians in the Gaza Strip, and in 2009, when he challenged the nerve of the new U.S. president, Barack Obama, to continue the fight against al-Qaeda.

Meanwhile, U.S. forces had continued to hunt for bin Laden, who was still thought possibly to be hiding either in Afghanistan or in the tribal regions of Pakistan near the border with Afghanistan. U.S. intelligence eventually located him in Pakistan, living in a secure compound in Abbottabad, a medium-sized city near Islamabad. On May 2, 2011, bin Laden was killed when a small U.S. force transported by helicopters raided the compound. His body, identified visually at the site of the raid, was taken out of Pakistan by U.S. forces for examination and DNA identification and soon after was given a sea burial. Hours after its confirmation, bin Laden's death was announced by Obama in a televised address. Several days after Obama's announcement, al-Qaeda released a statement publicly acknowledging bin Laden's death and vowing revenge.

In late May al-Qaeda released an audio message purportedly recorded by bin Laden shortly before he was killed. In the message, bin Laden praised the Tunisian and Egyptian uprisings of early 2011 and called on al-Qaeda followers to help people struggling against unjust governments.

# September 11 Attacks

The September 11 attacks, also called the 9/11 attacks, were a series of airline hijackings and suicide attacks committed by 19 militants associated with the Islamic extremist group al-Qaeda against targets in the United States, the deadliest terrorist attacks on American soil in U.S. history. The attacks against New York City and Washington, D.C., caused extensive death and destruction and triggered an enormous U.S. effort to combat terrorism. Some 2,750 people were killed in New York, 184 at the Pentagon, and 40 in Pennsylvania (where one of the hijacked planes crashed after the passengers attempted to retake the plane); all 19 terrorists died. Police and fire departments in New York were especially hard hit: hundreds had rushed to the scene of the attacks, and more than 400 police officers and firefighters were killed.

## The Plot

The September 11 attacks were precipitated in large part because Osama bin Laden, the leader of the militant Islamic organization al-Qaeda, held naive beliefs about the United States in the run-up to the attacks. Abu Walid al-Masri, an Egyptian who was a bin Laden associate in Afghanistan

# Ayman al-Zawahiri

Ayman al-Zawahiri (June 19, 1951– ) is an Egyptian physician and militant who became one of the major ideologues of al-Qaeda. Zawahiri was appointed leader of al-Qaeda in 2011.

Zawahiri was raised in Maʿādī, Egypt, several miles south of Cairo. Although his parents were from prominent families, Zawahiri and his siblings were raised in a relatively humble environment. Zawahiri was a pious youth. As a student, he was greatly influenced by the work of Sayyid Quṭb, an Egyptian writer who was one of the foremost figures in modern Sunni Islamic revivalism. By age 15 Zawahiri had established a group dedicated to the overthrow of the Egyptian government in favour of Islamic rule.

Zawahiri then studied at Cairo University's medical school, where he specialized in surgery; there he also continued his clandestine activities. He graduated in 1974 and then served for three years as an army surgeon. In 1980–81 he traveled as a relief worker with the Red Crescent to Peshawar, Pakistan, where he treated refugees affected by the Afghan War. During that time he made several cross-border trips into Afghanistan, where he witnessed the warfare firsthand.

After returning to Egypt, Zawahiri was one of several hundred militants arrested in the wake of the assassination of Pres. Anwar el-Sādāt in October 1981. Zawahiri was convicted of illegal arms possession and imprisoned for three years. During that time he was subjected to torture by intelligence officers interested in information about his contacts, an experience that intensified his militancy. In 1984 Zawahiri was released from prison. The following year he left for Saudi Arabia; from Jiddah he returned to Peshawar and then moved on to Afghanistan. During this period he became acquainted with Osama bin Laden, a wealthy Saudi who had joined the Afghan resistance to the Soviets, and in 1988 Zawahiri was present at the founding of al-Qaeda.

In the early 1990s Zawahiri assumed the leadership of the militant group Egyptian Islamic Jihad (thereafter better known as Islamic Jihad). Bin Laden had departed for Sudan in 1992, and Zawahiri ultimately joined him there. Sudan served as a base for the training of militants and for attacks on Egyptian targets, including attacks on government officials and on the Egyptian embassy in Pakistan. In June 1995 an unsuccessful attempt was made to assassinate Egyptian Pres. Hosnī Mubārak himself. Under international pressure, the Sudanese eventually expelled Zawahiri and bin Laden, along with their followers.

Zawahiri's next movements are unclear; he appears to have traveled to European countries that included Switzerland, Bulgaria, and the Netherlands. In late 1996 he was arrested by Russian officials while illegally crossing the border en route to Chechnya, where he planned to launch a new base for Islamic Jihad. Although he was jailed for six months, Russian agents were apparently unaware of his identity until after his release.

In 1998 Zawahiri and bin Laden forged a formal alliance, and in June 2001 Islamic Jihad and al-Qaeda were merged. Zawahiri was closely affiliated with both the bombing of the USS *Cole* in October 2000 and the attacks of Sept. 11, 2001. Zawahiri gradually became al-Qaeda's chief spokesman, issuing commentary on issues such as the U.S. invasion of Iraq in 2003 and the 2006 warfare between Hezbollah and Israel. In 2009 the U.S. Department of State determined that Zawahiri appeared to be al-Qaeda's leading decision maker, while bin Laden reportedly occupied figurehead status. Zawahiri assumed leadership of al-Qaeda in June 2011, following bin Laden's death during an American commando raid in Abbottabad, Pakistan, the previous month.

in the 1980s and '90s, explained that, in the years prior to the attacks, bin Laden became increasingly convinced that America was weak. "He believed that the United States was much weaker than some of those around him thought," Masri remembered, and "as evidence he referred to what happened to the United States in Beirut when the bombing of the Marines base led them to flee from Lebanon," referring to the destruction of the marine barracks there in 1983, which killed 241 American servicemen. Bin Laden believed that the United States was a "paper tiger," a belief shaped not just by America's departure from Lebanon following the marine barracks bombing but also by the withdrawal of American forces from Somalia in 1993, following the deaths of 18 U.S. servicemen in Mogadishu, and the American pullout from Vietnam in the 1970s.

The key operational planner of the September 11 attacks was Khalid Sheikh Mohammed (often referred to simply as "KSM" in the later *9/11 Commission Report* and in the media), who had spent his youth in Kuwait. Khalid Sheikh Mohammed became active in the Muslim Brotherhood, which he joined at age 16, and then he went to the United States to attend college, receiving a degree from North Carolina Agricultural and Technical State University in 1986. Afterward he traveled to Pakistan and then Afghanistan to wage jihad against the Soviet Union, which had launched an invasion against Afghanistan in 1979.

According to Yosri Fouda, a journalist at the Arabic-language cable television channel Al Jazeera who interviewed him in 2002, Khalid Sheikh Mohammed planned to blow up some dozen American planes in Asia during the mid-1990s, a plot (known as "Bojinka") that failed, "but the dream of Khalid Sheikh Mohammed never faded. And I think by putting his hand in the hands of bin Laden, he realized that now he stood a chance of bringing about his long awaited dream."

In 1996 Khalid Sheikh Mohammed met bin Laden in Tora Bora, Afghanistan. The 9-11 Commission (formally the National Commission on Terrorist Attacks Upon the United States), set up in 2002 by Pres. George W. Bush and the U.S. Congress to investigate the attacks of 2001, explained that it was then that Khalid Sheikh Mohammed "presented a proposal for an operation that would involve training pilots who would crash planes into buildings in the United States." Khalid Sheikh Mohammed dreamed up the tactical innovation of using hijacked planes to attack the United States; al-Qaeda provided the personnel, money, and logistical support to execute the operation; and bin Laden wove the attacks on New York and Washington into a larger strategic framework of attacking the "far enemy"—the United States—in order to bring about regime change across the Middle East.

The September 11 plot demonstrated that al-Qaeda was an organization of global reach. The plot played out across the globe with planning meetings in Malaysia, operatives taking flight lessons in the United States, coordination by plot leaders based in Hamburg, Germany, money transfers from Dubai, and recruitment of suicide operatives from countries around the Middle East—all activities that were ultimately overseen by al-Qaeda's leaders in Afghanistan.

Key parts of the September 11 plot took shape in Hamburg. Four of the key pilots and planners in the "Hamburg cell" who would take operational control of the September 11 attacks, including the lead hijacker Mohammed Atta, had a chance meeting on a train in Germany in 1999 with an Islamist militant who struck up a conversation with them about fighting jihad in Chechnya. The militant put the Hamburg cell in touch with an al-Qaeda operative living in Germany who explained that it was difficult to get to Chechnya at that time because many travelers were being detained in Georgia. He recommended they go to Afghanistan instead.

Although Afghanistan was critical to the rise of al-Qaeda, it was the experience that some of the plotters acquired in the West that made them simultaneously more zealous and better equipped to carry out the attacks. Three of the four plotters who would pilot the hijacked planes on September

11 and one of the key planners, Ramzi Binalshibh, became more radical while living in Hamburg. Some combination of perceived or real discrimination, alienation, and homesickness seems to have turned them all in a more militant direction. Increasingly cutting themselves off from the outside world, they gradually radicalized each other, and eventually the friends decided to wage battle in bin Laden's global jihad, setting off for Afghanistan in 1999 in search of al-Qaeda.

Atta and the other members of the Hamburg group arrived in Afghanistan in 1999 right at the moment that the September 11 plot was beginning to take shape. Bin Laden and his military commander Muhammad Atef realized that Atta and his fellow Western-educated jihadists were far better suited to lead the attacks on Washington and New York than the men they had already recruited, leading bin Laden to appoint Atta to head the operation.

The hijackers, most of whom were from Saudi Arabia, established themselves in the United States, many well in advance of the attacks. They traveled in small groups, and some of them received commercial flight training.

Throughout his stay in the United States, Atta kept Binalshibh updated on the plot's progress via e-mail. To cloak his activities, Atta wrote the messages as if he were writing to his girlfriend "Jenny," using innocuous code to inform Binalshibh that they were almost complete in their training and readiness for the attacks. Atta wrote in one message, "The first semester commences in three weeks...Nineteen certificates for private education and four exams." The referenced 19 "certificates" were code that identified the 19 al-Qaeda hijackers, while the four "exams" identified the targets of the attacks.

In the early morning of August 29, 2001, Atta called Binalshibh and said he had a riddle that he was trying to solve: "Two sticks, a dash and a cake with a stick down—

what is it?" After considering the question, Binalshibh realized that Atta was telling him that the attacks would occur in two weeks—the two sticks being the number 11 and the cake with a stick down a 9. Putting it together, it meant that the attacks would occur on 11-9, or 11 September (in most countries the day precedes the month in numeric dates, but in the United States the month precedes the day; hence, it was 9-11 in the United States). On September 5 Binalshibh left Germany for Pakistan. Once there he sent a messenger to Afghanistan to inform bin Laden about both the day of the attack and its scope.

## The Attacks

On Sept. 11, 2001, groups of attackers boarded four domestic aircraft at three East Coast airports, and soon after take-off they disabled the crews, some of whom may have been stabbed with box cutters the hijackers were secreting. The hijackers then took control of the aircraft, all large and bound for the West Coast with full loads of fuel. At 8:46 AM the first plane, American Airlines Flight 11, which had originated from Boston, was piloted into the north tower of the World Trade Center in New York City. Most observers construed this initially to be an accident involving a small commuter plane. The second plane, United Airlines Flight 175, also from Boston, struck the south tower 17 minutes later. At this point there was no doubt that the United States was under attack. Each structure was badly damaged by the impact and erupted into flames. Office workers who were trapped above the points of impact in some cases leapt to their deaths rather than face the infernos now raging inside the towers. The third plane, American Airlines Flight 77, taking off from Dulles Airport near Washington, D.C., struck the southwest side of the Pentagon (just outside the city) at 9:37 AM, touching off a fire in

*The aftermath of the terrorist attack on the World Trade Center in New York on Sept. 11, 2001.* Henny Ray Abrams/AFP/Getty Images

that section of the structure. Minutes later the Federal Aviation Authority ordered a nationwide ground stop, and within the next hour (at 10:03 AM) the fourth aircraft, United Airlines Flight 93 from Newark, N.J., crashed near Shanksville in the Pennsylvania countryside after its passengers—informed of events via cellular phone—attempted to overpower their assailants.

At 9:59 AM the World Trade Center's heavily damaged south tower collapsed, and the north tower fell 29 minutes later. Clouds of smoke and debris quickly filled the streets of Lower Manhattan. Office workers and residents ran in panic as they tried to outpace the billowing debris clouds. A number of other buildings adjacent to the twin towers suffered serious damage, and several subsequently fell. Fires at the World Trade Center site smoldered for more than three months.

Rescue operations began almost immediately as the country and the world sought to come to grips with the enormity of the losses. Nearly 3,000 people had perished: some 2,750 people in New York, 184 at the Pentagon, and 40 in Pennsylvania; all 19 terrorists also died. Included in the total in New York City were more than 400 police officers and firefighters who had lost their lives after rushing to the scene and into the towers.

On the morning of September 11, President Bush had been visiting a second-grade classroom in Sarasota, Fla., when he was informed that a plane had flown into the World Trade Center. A little later Andrew Card, his chief of staff, whispered in the president's right ear: "A second plane hit the second tower. America is under attack." To keep the president out of harm's way, Bush subsequently hopscotched across the country on Air Force One, landing in Washington, D.C., the evening of the attacks. At 8:30 PM Bush addressed the nation from the Oval Office in a speech that laid out a key doctrine of his administration's future foreign policy: "We will make no distinction between the terrorists who committed these acts and those who harbor them."

On September 14 Bush visited "Ground Zero," the smoking pile of debris of what remained of the World Trade Center and the thousands who had perished there. Standing on top of a wrecked fire truck, Bush grabbed a bullhorn to address the rescue workers working feverishly to find any survivors. When one of the workers said that he could not hear what the president was saying, Bush made one of the most memorable remarks of his presidency: "I can hear you. The rest of the world hears you. And the people who knocked these buildings down will hear from all of us soon."

Bush's robust response to the attacks drove his poll ratings from 55 percent favourable before September 11 to 90 percent in the days after, the highest ever recorded for a president.

## The Aftermath

The emotional distress caused by the attacks—particularly the collapse of the twin towers, New York City's most visible landmark—was overwhelming. Unlike the relatively isolated site of the Pearl Harbor attack of 1941, to which the September 11 events were soon compared, the World Trade Center lay at the heart of one of the world's largest cities. Hundreds of thousands of people witnessed the attacks firsthand (many onlookers photographed events or recorded them with video cameras), and millions watched the tragedy unfold live on television. In the days that followed September 11, the footage of the attacks was replayed in the media countless times, as were the scenes of throngs of people, stricken with grief, gathering at Ground Zero, some with photos of missing loved ones, seeking some hint of their fate.

Moreover, world markets were badly shaken. The towers were at the heart of New York's financial district, and damage to Lower Manhattan's infrastructure, combined with fears of stock market panic, kept New York markets closed for four trading days. Markets afterward suffered record losses. The attacks also stranded tens of thousands of people throughout the United States, as U.S. airspace remained closed for commercial aviation until September 13, and normal service, with more rigid security measures, did not resume for several days.

The September 11 attacks were an enormous tactical success for al-Qaeda. The strikes were well coordinated and hit multiple targets in the heart of the enemy, and the attacks were magnified by being broadcast around the world to an audience of untold millions. The September 11 "propaganda of the deed" took place in the media capital of the world, which ensured the widest possible coverage of the event. Not since television viewers had watched the abduction and murder of Israeli athletes during the Munich Olympics in 1972 had a massive global audience witnessed a terrorist attack unfold in real time. If al-Qaeda had been a largely unknown organization before September 11, in the days after it became a household name.

After the attacks of September 11, countries allied with the United States rallied to its support, perhaps best symbolized by the French newspaper *Le Monde*'s headline, "We are all Americans now." Even in Iran thousands gathered in the capital, Tehrān, for a candlelight vigil.

Evidence gathered by the United States soon convinced most governments that the Islamic militant group al-Qaeda was responsible for the attacks. The group had been implicated in previous terrorist strikes against Americans, and bin Laden had made numerous anti-American statements. Al-Qaeda was headquartered in Afghanistan and had forged a close relationship with that country's ruling Taliban militia, which subsequently refused U.S. demands to extradite bin Laden and to terminate al-Qaeda activity there.

For the first time in its history, the North Atlantic Treaty Organization (NATO) invoked Article 5, allowing its members to respond collectively in self-defense, and on October 7 the U.S. and allied military forces launched an attack against Afghanistan. Within months thousands of militants were killed or captured, and Taliban and al-Qaeda leaders were driven into hiding. In addition, the U.S. government exerted great effort to track down other al-Qaeda agents and sympathizers throughout the world and made combating terrorism the focus of U.S. foreign policy. Meanwhile, security measures within the United States were tightened considerably at such places as airports, government buildings, and sports venues. To help facilitate the domestic response, Congress quickly passed the USA PATRIOT Act (the Uniting and Strengthening America by Providing Appropriate Tools Required to Intercept and Obstruct Terrorism Act of 2001), which significantly but temporarily expanded the search and surveillance powers of the Federal Bureau of Investigation (FBI) and other law-enforcement agencies. Additionally, a cabinet-level Department of Homeland Security was established.

Despite their success in causing widespread destruction and death, the September 11 attacks were a strategic failure for al-Qaeda. Following September 11, al-Qaeda—whose name in Arabic means "the base"—lost the best base it ever had in Afghanistan. Later some in al-Qaeda's leadership—including those who, like Egyptian Saif al-Adel, had initially opposed the attacks—tried to spin the Western intervention in Afghanistan as a victory for al-Qaeda. Al-Adel, one of the group's military commanders, explained in an interview four years later that the strikes on New York and Washington were part of a far-reaching and visionary plan to provoke the United States into some ill-advised actions: "Such strikes will force the person to carry out random acts and provoke him to make serious and sometimes fatal mistakes....The first reaction was the invasion of Afghanistan."

But there is not a shred of evidence that in the weeks before September 11 al-Qaeda's leaders made any plans for an American invasion of Afghanistan. Instead, they prepared only for possible U.S. cruise missile attacks or air strikes by evacuating their training camps. Also, the overthrow of the Taliban hardly constituted an American "mistake"—the first and only regime in the modern Muslim world that ruled according to al-Qaeda's rigid precepts was toppled, and with it was lost an entire country that al-Qaeda had once enjoyed as a safe haven. And in the wake of the fall of the Taliban, al-Qaeda was unable to recover anything like the status it once had as a terrorist organization with considerable sway over Afghanistan.

Bin Laden disastrously misjudged the possible U.S. responses to the September 11 attacks, which he believed would take one of two forms: an eventual retreat from the

Middle East along the lines of the U.S. pullout from Somalia in 1993 or another ineffectual round of cruise missile attacks similar to those that followed al-Qaeda's bombings of American embassies in Kenya and Tanzania in 1998. Neither of these two scenarios happened. The U.S. campaign against the Taliban was conducted with pinpoint strikes from American airpower, tens of thousands of Northern Alliance forces (a loose coalition of *mujahideen* militias that maintained control of a small section of northern Afghanistan), and more than 300 U.S. Special Forces soldiers on the ground working with 110 officers from the Central Intelligence Agency (CIA). In November, just two months after the September 11 attacks, the Taliban fell to the Northern Alliance and the United States. Still, it was just the beginning of what would become the longest war in U.S. history, as the United States tried to prevent the return of the Taliban and their al-Qaeda allies.

In December 2001, faced with the problem of where to house prisoners as the Taliban fell, the administration decided to hold them at Guantánamo Bay, which the U.S. had been leasing from Cuba since 1903. As Secretary of Defense Donald Rumsfeld put it on Dec. 27, 2001, "I would characterize Guantánamo Bay, Cuba, as the least worst place we could have selected." Guantánamo was attractive to administration officials because they believed it placed the detainees outside the reach of American laws, such as the right to appeal their imprisonment, yet it was only 90 miles (145 km) off the coast of Florida, making it accessible to the various agencies that would need to travel there to extract information from what was believed to be a population of hundreds of dangerous terrorists. Eventually, some 800 prisoners would be held there, although the prison population was reduced to less than 175 by the time of the 10th anniversary of the September 11 attacks.

In his State of the Union speech on Jan. 29, 2002, President Bush laid out a new doctrine of preemptive war, which went well beyond the long-established principle that the United States would go to war to prevent an adversary launching an attack that imminently threatened the country. Bush declared: "I will not wait on events while dangers gather. I will not stand by as peril draws closer and closer. The United States of America will not permit the world's most dangerous regimes to threaten us with the world's most destructive weapons."

Bush identified those dangerous regimes as an "axis of evil" that included Iran, Iraq, and North Korea. At the graduation ceremony for West Point cadets on June 1, 2002, Bush elaborated on his preemptive war doctrine, saying to the assembled soon-to-be graduates and their families, "If we wait for threats to fully materialize, we will have waited too long." Bush believed that there would be a "demonstration effect" in destroying Ṣaddam Ḥussein's regime in Iraq that would deter groups like al-Qaeda or indeed anyone else who might be inclined to attack the United States. Undersecretary of Defense Douglas J. Feith later explained, "What we did after 9/11 was look broadly at the international terrorist network from which the next attack on the United States might come. And we did not focus narrowly only on the people who were specifically responsible for 9/11. Our main goal was preventing the next attack."

Thus, though there was no evidence that Ṣaddam Ḥussein's government in Iraq had collaborated with al-Qaeda in the September 11 attacks, the United States prepared for conflict against Iraq in its global war against terror, broadly defined.

On March 19, 2003, on the eve of the invasion of Iraq, President Bush issued the order for war: "For the peace of the world and the benefit and freedom of the Iraqi people, I hereby give the order to execute Operation Iraqi Freedom. May God bless the troops."

On March 20 the American-led invasion of Iraq began. Within three weeks U.S. forces controlled Baghdad, and the famous pictures of the massive statue of Ṣaddam Ḥussein being toppled from its plinth were broadcast around the world.

## The September 11 Commission and Its Findings

In 2002 President Bush had appointed a commission to look into the September 11 attacks, and two years later it issued its final report. The commission found that the key pre-September 11 failure at the CIA was its not adding to the State Department's "watch list" two of the "muscle" hijackers (who were trained to restrain the passengers on the plane), the suspected al-Qaeda militants Nawaf al-Hazmi and Khalid al-Mihdhar. The CIA had been tracking Hazmi and Mihdhar since they attended a terrorist summit meeting in Kuala Lumpur, Malaysia, on Jan. 5, 2000. The failure to watch-list the two al-Qaeda suspects with the Department of State meant that they entered the United States under their real names with ease. On Jan. 15, 2000, 10 days after the Malaysian meeting, Hazmi and Mihdhar flew into Los Angeles. The CIA also did not alert the FBI about the identities of the suspected terrorists, which could have helped the bureau locate them once they were inside the United States. According to the commission, this was the failure of not just a few employees at the CIA but a large number of CIA officers and analysts. Some 50 to 60 CIA employees read cables about the two al-Qaeda suspects without taking any action. Some of those officers knew that one of the al-Qaeda suspects had a visa for the United States, and by May 2001 some knew that the other suspect had flown to Los Angeles.

The soon-to-be hijackers would not have been difficult to find in California if their names had been known to law enforcement. Under their real names they rented an apartment, obtained driver's licenses, opened bank accounts, purchased a car, and took flight lessons at a local school; Mihdhar even listed his name in the local phone directory.

It was only on Aug. 24, 2001, as a result of questions raised by a CIA officer on assignment at the FBI, that the two al-Qaeda suspects were watch-listed and their names communicated to the FBI. Even then the FBI sent out only a "Routine" notice requesting an investigation of Mihdhar. A few weeks later Hazmi and Mihdhar were two of the hijackers on the American Airlines flight that plunged into the Pentagon.

The CIA inspector general concluded that "informing the FBI and good operational follow-through by CIA and FBI might have resulted in surveillance of both al-Mihdhar and al-Hazmi. Surveillance, in turn, would have had the potential to yield information on flight training, financing, and links to others who were complicit in the 9/11 attacks."

The key failure at the FBI was the handling of the Zacarias Moussaoui case. Moussaoui, a French citizen of Moroccan descent, was attending flight school in the summer of 2001 in Minnesota, where he attracted attention from instructors because he had little knowledge of flying and did not behave like a typical aviation student. The flight school contacted the FBI, and on August 16 Moussaoui was arrested on a visa overstay charge. Although Moussaoui was not the "20th hijacker," as was widely reported later, he had received money from one of the September 11 coordinators, Ramzi Binalshibh, and by his own account was going to take part in a second wave of al-Qaeda attacks following the assaults on New York and Washington.

The FBI agent in Minneapolis who handled Moussaoui's case believed that he might have been planning to hijack a plane, and the agent was also concerned that Moussaoui had traveled to Pakistan, which was a red flag as militants often used the country as a transit point to travel to terrorist training camps in Afghanistan. On August 23 (or 24, according to some reports) CIA director George Tenet was told about the case in a briefing titled "Islamic Extremist Learns to Fly." But FBI headquarters determined that there was not sufficient "probable cause" of a crime for the Minneapolis office to conduct a search of Moussaoui's computer hard drive and belongings. Such a search would have turned up his connection to Binalshibh, according to Republican Sen. Charles Grassley, a leading member of the Senate Judiciary Committee, which has oversight of the FBI. The 9-11 Commission also concluded that "a maximum U.S. effort to investigate Moussaoui conceivably could have unearthed his connection to Binalshibh."

## The Hunt for bin Laden

In September 2001 President Bush announced that he wanted Osama bin Laden captured—dead or alive—and a $25 million bounty was eventually issued for information leading to the killing or capture of bin Laden. Bin Laden evaded capture, however, including in December 2001, when he was tracked by U.S. forces to the mountains of Tora Bora in eastern Afghanistan. Bin Laden's trail subsequently went cold, and he was thought to be living somewhere in the Afghanistan-Pakistan tribal regions.

U.S. intelligence eventually located him in Pakistan, living in the garrison city of Abbottabad, and in the early morning hours of May 2, 2011, on orders from U.S. Pres. Barack Obama, a small team of U.S. Navy SEALs assaulted his compound and shot and killed the al-Qaeda leader.

# Al-Qaeda in Iraq

Al-Qaeda in Iraq, also called al-Qaeda in Mesopotamia, is a militant Sunni network, active in Iraq after the U.S.-led invasion of 2003, comprising Iraqi and foreign fighters opposed to the U.S. occupation and the Shīʿite-dominated Iraqi government.

Al-Qaeda in Iraq first appeared in 2004 when Abū Muṣʿab al-Zarqāwī, a Jordanian-born militant already leading insurgent attacks in Iraq, formed an alliance with al-Qaeda, pledging his group's allegiance to Osama bin Laden in return for bin Laden's endorsement as the leader of al-Qaeda's franchise in Iraq. Al-Zarqāwī, who quickly came to be regarded as one of the most destructive militants in Iraq, organized a wave of attacks, often suicide bombings, that targeted security forces, government institutions, and Iraqi civilians. Intending to deepen the sectarian conflict at the heart of the Iraq War, al-Qaeda in Iraq especially targeted Iraqi Shīʿites, sometimes during religious processions or at Shīʿite mosques and shrines. A 2006 attack widely attributed to al-Qaeda in Iraq destroyed the golden dome of Al-ʿAskariyyah Mosque in Sāmarrāʾ, one of Shīʿism's holiest mosques, amplifying the existing cycle of violent retribution and provoking some of the worst sectarian violence of the post-invasion period.

Al-Qaeda in Iraq remained active even after al-Zarqāwī was killed by U.S. forces in 2006. The organization was severely weakened in 2007, however, after Sunni tribes paid by the United States began to form militias known as "Awakening Councils" to expel al-Qaeda in Iraq from their territories. Many of those groups had previously participated in the insurgency but were alienated by al-Qaeda in Iraq's often brutal treatment of civilians, as well as its efforts to replace local tribal power structures with an al-Qaeda-governed state. Although that reversal, coupled with an increasingly successful effort by U.S. and Iraqi forces to kill al-Qaeda in Iraq leaders, greatly diminished the organization's power, the network continued to operate on a reduced scale, targeting Shī'ites, Christians, members of the Awakening Councils, and the Iraqi government.

# Al-Qaeda in the Arabian Peninsula

This Yemen-based militant group was formed in 2009 by the merger of radical networks in Saudi Arabia and Yemen and linked to attacks in Yemen, Saudi Arabia, and the United States.

After a series of deadly al-Qaeda attacks on U.S. and other Western targets in Saudi Arabia and Yemen between 2000 and 2004, militant Islamic networks in the region were weakened when a number of their local leaders were killed or captured by security forces. Islamic militancy revived in Yemen in 2006, however, when 23 al-Qaeda militants escaped from a prison in Sanaa. Two of the escapees—Nāṣir al-Waḥ ayshī, a former aide to al-Qaeda head Osama bin Laden, and Qāsim al-Raymī—began to rebuild militant networks and to attack targets in Yemen. In January 2009 they announced the formation of a new organization that incorporated Yemeni and Saudi fighters into its leadership under the name al-Qaeda in the Arabian Peninsula. In August 2009 that group was linked to a bold attempt to assassinate Muḥammad bin Nayif, the chief of counterterrorism in Saudi Arabia.

Another major attempt followed on Dec. 25, 2009, when a Nigerian AQAP militant tried to detonate explosives hidden in his clothes while aboard an international flight that was arriving in the United States—an attack that AQAP leaders claimed as retaliation for U.S.-supported Yemeni air strikes targeting the group in Yemen. In October 2010 security officials foiled another AQAP attack, finding and defusing explosives hidden in air freight packages on flights bound for the United States.

AQAP received media attention for its suspected ties to the radical imam Anwār al-Awlākī, a U.S. citizen of Yemeni descent thought to have hidden with the group in Yemen. Awlākī, who was killed in a U.S. air strike in Yemen in September 2011, is thought to have personally provided guidance and encouragement to people involved in acts of terrorism, including three of the Sept. 11, 2001, hijackers as well as Nidal Hasan, a U.S. Army psychiatrist charged with killing 13 people in a 2009 shooting spree at an army base in Texas.

Public statements made by AQAP appealed to popular dissatisfaction with Middle Eastern governments, condemning the rulers of Saudi Arabia and Yemen as corrupt and servile to Western interests. In Yemen the group blamed the administration of Pres. ʿAlī ʿAbd Allāh Ṣāliḥ for a number of problems that were major sources of public discontent, including endemic poverty, water shortages, and rising prices for basic goods.

In 2011 AQAP found itself in control of a swath of territory centred in the Abyan and Shabwah governorates when government forces were withdrawn from the area to confront an uprising against the Ṣāliḥ regime. Under Ṣāliḥ's successor, ʿAbd Rabbuh Manṣūr Hadī, an offensive to retake the area was launched in 2012 with the support of the United States, which also carried out series of air strikes by unmanned drones targeting suspected militants. By mid-2012 Yemeni forces had retaken most of the areas formerly under AQAP's control.

# Al-Qaeda in the Islamic Maghrib

Al-Qaeda in the Islamic Maghrib is an Algeria-based Islamic militant group, active in North Africa and the Sahel region. It was founded as the GSPC (Salafist Group for Preaching and Combat) in 1998 by a former member of the Armed Islamic Group (Groupe Islamique Armé; GIA), an Islamic militant group that participated in Algeria's civil war in the 1990s. The GSPC continued to fight the Algerian government but renounced the killing of Algerian civilians, a common GIA practice. The GSPC took over some GIA networks in the Sahel and the Sahara, where it generated revenue by smuggling. In 2003 international attention was focused on the GSPC when it took 32 European tourists hostage in the Sahara. Some of the hostages were freed by the Algerian army; others were released, reportedly in exchange for a ransom payment. Also in 2003 the GSPC's leader and founder, Ḥasan Ḥaṭṭāb, was apparently forced out of the organization by the more radical members Abdelmalek Droukdel (also known as Abū Musʻab al-Wadūd) and Nabīl Saḥrāwī. After Saḥrāwī was killed by Algerian forces in 2004, Droukdel took over leadership, steering the GSPC toward a stronger affiliation with Osama bin Laden's al-Qaeda network. As the group sought recognition from al-Qaeda's leaders, it became more active outside Algeria, channeling fighters to the Iraq War and launching an attack on a military post in Mauritania. In 2006 Droukdel announced that the GSPC had merged with al-Qaeda, and in 2007 the organization changed its name to al-Qaeda in the Islamic Maghrib (AQIM).

In 2007, after several months of small attacks in mostly rural areas of Algeria, AQIM struck several high-profile targets in Algiers. A three-pronged suicide attack in April penetrated heavy security in Algiers, striking the Government Palace, where many senior officials' offices were located, as well as a police station and nearby gendarmerie station, killing 33. In December coordinated blasts in Algiers outside the Constitutional Council building and at the offices of the United Nations (UN) killed more than 40 people, including 17 UN workers.

AQIM also began to operate more aggressively across national borders in the western Sahel, running smuggling networks and abducting Westerners. Those operations led to clashes between AQIM and the armies of Mauritania, Mali, and Niger, which received military and counterterrorism assistance from Europe and the United States.

# Taliban

The Taliban is an ultraconservative political and religious faction that emerged in Afghanistan in the mid-1990s following the withdrawal of Soviet troops, the collapse of Afghanistan's communist regime, and the subsequent breakdown in civil order. The faction took its name from its membership, which consisted largely of students trained in *madrasahs* (Islamic religious schools) that were established for Afghan refugees in the 1980s in northern Pakistan.

The Taliban emerged as a force for social order in 1994 in the southern Afghan province of Kandahār and quickly subdued the local warlords who controlled the south of the country. By late 1996, popular support for the Taliban among Afghanistan's southern Pashtun ethnic group, as well as assistance from conservative Islamic elements abroad, had enabled the faction to seize the capital, Kabul, and gain effective control of the country. Resistance to the Taliban continued, however, particularly among non-Pashtun ethnic groups—namely, the Tajik, the Uzbek, and the Ḥazāra— in the north, west, and central parts of the country, who saw the power of the predominantly Pashtun Taliban as a continuation of the traditional Pashtun hegemony of the country. By 2001 the Taliban controlled all but a small section of northern Afghanistan.

World opinion, however, largely disapproved of the Taliban's social policies—including the near-total exclusion of

*Taliban fighters.* Robert Nickelsberg/Time & Life Pictures/Getty Images

women from public life (including employment and education), the systematic destruction of non-Islamic artistic relics (as occurred in the town of Bamiyan), and the implementation of harsh criminal punishments—and only a few countries recognized the regime. More significant was the fact that the Taliban allowed Afghanistan to be a haven for Islamic militants from throughout the world, including an exiled Saudi Arabian,

# Mohammad Omar

Mohammad Omar, also called Mullah Omar (born *c.* 1950–62?) is an Afghan militant and leader of the Taliban who was the emir of Afghanistan (1996–2001). Mullah Omar's refusal to extradite al-Qaeda leader Osama bin Laden prompted the U.S. invasion of Afghanistan in 2001 that overthrew the Taliban government there.

Biographical details about Mullah Omar are sparse and conflicting. He is an ethnic Pashtun of the Ghilzay branch. Reportedly, he was born near Kandahār, Afghanistan. He is believed to be illiterate and—aside from his *madrasah* studies—to have had minimal schooling. He fought with the *mujahideen* against the Soviets during the Afghan War (1978–92); during that time he suffered the loss of his right eye in an explosion.

After the Soviet withdrawal, Mullah Omar established and taught at a small village *madrasah* in the province of Kandahār. The end of the war did not bring calm, however, and political and ethnic violence escalated thereafter. Claiming to have had a vision instructing him to restore peace, Mullah Omar led a group of *madrasah* students in the takeover of cities throughout the mid-1990s, including Kandahār, Herāt, Kabul, and Mazār-e Sharīf. In 1996 a *shūrā* (council) recognized Mullah Omar as *amīr al-mu'minīn* ("commander of the faithful"), a deeply significant title in the Muslim world that had been in disuse since the abolition of the caliphate in 1924. This designation also made him emir of Afghanistan, which from October 1997 until the fall of the Taliban was known as the Islamic Emirate of Afghanistan. Mullah Omar marked the occasion by removing what was held to be the cloak of the Prophet Muhammad from the mosque in Kandahār where it was housed and donning the relic, effectively symbolizing himself as Muhammad's successor. The swift takeover of Afghanistan by the Taliban under Mullah Omar is believed to have been funded at least in part by bin Laden, who had moved his base to Afghanistan after his expulsion from Sudan in the mid-1990s.

Under Mullah Omar's leadership, Pashtun social codes were paramount, and strict Islamic principles were enforced. Education and employment for women all but ceased; capital punishment for transgressions such as adultery and conversion away from Islam was enacted; and music, television, and other forms of popular entertainment were prohibited. Among his most infamous decisions was an order to demolish the colossal Buddha statues at Bamiyan, culturally significant relics of Afghanistan's pre-Islamic history. To the outspoken regret of the international community, they were destroyed in 2001.

In the wake of al-Qaeda's Sept. 11, 2001, attacks on New York City and Washington, D.C., Mullah Omar's refusal to extradite bin Laden prompted the United States to launch a series of military operations in Afghanistan. The Taliban government was overthrown, and Mullah Omar fled; his location was undetermined.

Mullah Omar was long notoriously reclusive. Meetings with non-Muslims or with Westerners were almost never granted, and it is unclear whether any of the photographs that purportedly depict him are authentic—circumstances that make his apprehension even more difficult. At the end of the first decade of the 21st century, it was believed that Mullah Omar continued to direct Taliban operations from the sanctuary of Pakistan, although the Taliban denied that supposition.

Osama bin Laden, who, as leader of al-Qaeda, stood accused of organizing numerous terrorist attacks against American interests. The Taliban's refusal to extradite bin Laden to the United States following the attacks on the World Trade Center in New York City and the Pentagon outside Washington, D.C., on Sept. 11, 2001, prompted a military confrontation with the United States and allied powers. The Taliban was subsequently driven from power.

Taliban insurgency against U.S. and NATO forces continued in the years following the Taliban's ouster. The Taliban funded its efforts in large part through a thriving opium trade, which reached record levels several years after the fall of the Taliban. Although expelled from Kandahār by the invasion, Taliban leader Mullah Mohammad Omar reportedly continued to direct the insurgency from an unknown location; he was thought by some to be in Pakistan, although the Taliban denied this.

# Kurdistan Workers' Party (PKK)

The Kurdistan Workers' Party (PKK) was a militant Kurdish nationalist organization founded by Abdullah ("Apo") Öcalan in the late 1970s. Although the group initially espoused demands for the establishment of an independent Kurdish state, its stated aims were later tempered to calls for greater Kurdish autonomy.

Although the Kurdish population has for centuries been concentrated over large parts of what are now eastern Turkey, northern Iraq, and western Iran, as well as smaller parts of northern Syria and Armenia, it never achieved nation-state status. Kurdish aspirations for self-determination were often ill-received, and Kurds historically experienced persecution or pressure to assimilate in their respective countries; the Kurds of Turkey received unsympathetic treatment at the hands of the government.

Major social changes in Turkey contributed to the proliferation and radicalization of Kurdish nationalist groups in that country in the 1960s and '70s. The PKK was among the various groups that emerged, formally founded by Öcalan in late 1978 as a Marxist organization dedicated to the creation of an independent Kurdistan. At its foundation, the PKK distinguished itself by its social makeup—its members were drawn largely from the lower classes—and its radicalism; the group espoused violence as a tenet central to its cause and demonstrated early its willingness to employ force against Kurds perceived as government collaborators and against rival Kurdish organizations.

In 1979 Öcalan departed Turkey for Syria, where he established connections with militant Palestinian organizations. In the wake of the 1980 coup in Turkey, portions of the PKK were dispersed abroad to neighbouring countries, including Lebanon and Syria, where they received training supported by the contacts Öcalan had made with Palestinian groups there.

In the early 1980s, favourable relations with the Iraqi Kurdistan Democratic Party allowed for the movement of PKK militants into camps in northern Iraq, from which the PKK launched an armed campaign against Turkey in 1984. The PKK subsequently perpetrated frequent acts of terrorism and conducted guerrilla operations against a range of targets, including government installations and officials, Turks living in the country's Kurdish regions, Kurds accused of collaborating with the government, foreigners, and Turkish diplomatic missions abroad.

During the 1980s and '90s, PKK attacks and reprisals by the Turkish government led to a state of virtual war in eastern Turkey. In the 1990s Turkish troops also attacked PKK bases in the so-called safe havens of Iraqi Kurdistan in northern Iraq (created in the wake of the Persian Gulf War [1990–91]), first from the air and then with ground forces. In February 1999 Öcalan was captured in Nairobi and flown to Turkey, where in June he was convicted of treason and sentenced to death; following Turkey's abolition of the death penalty in August 2002, however, his sentence was commuted to life in prison the following October. After the imprisonment of its leader, PKK activities were sharply curtailed; the group underwent several name changes and attempted to restructure its image before resuming guerrilla activities in 2004.

The group was thought to be the source of a number of subsequent attacks in southeastern Turkey over the next few years. In October 2007 the Turkish parliament approved military action for one year against PKK targets across the border in Iraq; a series of strikes began in December, and a ground incursion was initiated in February 2008.

Beginning in 2009, Turkish officials and PKK leaders held secret talks to explore options for peace. Negotiations faltered when the repatriation of 34 PKK fighters and refugees to Turkey in late 2009 provoked a public celebration among PKK supporters, angering Turkish officials. The negotiations continued for several more rounds before ending in 2011 without progress. During that time Turkish authorities continued to arrest members of legal Kurdish parties, usually on charges of having belonged to terrorist groups. Violence increased after talks ended, reaching its highest level in more than a decade.

A new round of peace negotiations between Turkey and the PKK was announced in December 2012. From early on, the new talks showed more promise than the ones that had ended in 2011. In March 2013 the PKK released eight Turkish hostages, and Öcalan, still in Turkish custody, announced his support for a cease-fire.

## Muslim Brotherhood

The Muslim Brotherhood is a religio-political organization founded in 1928 at Ismailia, Egypt, by Ḥasan al-Bannāʿ. It advocated a return to the Qur'ān and the Hadith as guidelines for a healthy modern Islamic society. The Brotherhood spread rapidly throughout Egypt, Sudan, Syria, Palestine, Lebanon, and North Africa. Although figures of Brotherhood member-ship are variable, it is estimated that at its height in the late 1940s it may have had some 500,000 members.

Initially centred on religious and educational programs, the Muslim Brotherhood was seen as providing much-needed social services, and in the 1930s its membership grew swiftly. In the late 1930s the Brotherhood began to politicize its outlook, and, as an opponent of Egypt's ruling Wafd party, during World War II it organized popular protests against the government. An armed branch organized in the early 1940s was subsequently linked to a number of violent acts, including bombings and political assassinations, and it appears that the armed element of the group began to escape Ḥasan al-Bannā''s control. The Brotherhood responded to the government's attempts to dissolve the group by assassinating Prime Minister Maḥmūd Fahmī al-Nuqrāshī in December 1948. Ḥasan al-Bannā' himself was assassinated shortly thereafter; many believe his death was at the behest of the government.

With the advent of the revolutionary regime in Egypt in 1952, the Brotherhood retreated underground. An attempt to assassinate Egyptian Pres. Gamal Abdel Nasser in Alexandria on October 26, 1954, led to the Muslim Brotherhood's forcible suppression. Six of its leaders were tried and executed for treason, and many others were imprisoned. Among those imprisoned was writer Sayyid Quṭb, who authored a number of books during the course of his imprisonment; among these works was *Signposts in the Road*, which would become a template for modern Sunni militancy. Although he was released from prison in 1964, he was arrested again the following year and executed shortly thereafter. In the 1960s and '70s the Brotherhood's activities remained largely clandestine.

In the 1980s the Muslim Brotherhood experienced a renewal as part of the general upsurge of religious activity in Islamic countries. The Brotherhood's new adherents aimed to reorganize society and government according to Islamic doctrines, and they were vehemently anti-Western. An uprising by the Brotherhood in the Syrian city of Ḥamāh in February 1982 was crushed by the government of Ḥafiz al-Assad at a cost of perhaps 25,000 lives. The Brotherhood revived in Egypt and Jordan in the same period, and, beginning in the late 1980s, it emerged to compete in legislative elections in those countries.

In Egypt the participation of the Muslim Brotherhood in parliamentary elections there in the 1980s was followed by its boycott of the elections of 1990, when it joined most of the country's opposition in protesting electoral strictures. Although the group itself remained formally banned, in the 2000 elections Brotherhood supporters running as independent candidates were able to win 17 seats, making it the largest opposition bloc in the parliament. In 2005, again running as independents, the Brotherhood and its supporters captured 88 seats in spite of efforts by Pres. Ḥosnī Mubārak's administration to restrict voting in the group's strongholds. Its unexpected success in 2005 was met with additional restrictions and arrests, and the Brotherhood opted to boycott the 2008 local elections. In the 2010 parliamentary elections the Mubārak administration continued to restrict the Muslim Brotherhood by arresting members and barring voters in areas where the organization had strong support. After Mubārak's National Democratic Party won 209 out of 211 seats in the first round of voting, effectively eliminating the Muslim Brotherhood from the parliament, the organization boycotted the second round.

In January 2011 a nonreligious youth protest movement against the Mubārak regime appeared in Egypt. After hesitating briefly, the Muslim Brotherhood's senior leadership endorsed the movement and called on its members to participate in demonstrations. The protests soon forced Mubārak to step down as president in February, clearing the way for the Muslim Brotherhood's open participation in Egyptian politics. Brotherhood leaders outlined a cautious political strategy for the group, stating that they would not seek a majority in the legislature or nominate a candidate for president. In May, however, a senior member of the Muslim Brotherhood, Abdel-Moneim Abul-Fotouh, announced his intention to run for president; he was later expelled from the organization.

In late April 2011 the Muslim Brotherhood founded a political party called the Freedom and Justice Party and applied for official recognition from the Egyptian interim government. Leaders of the Freedom and Justice Party stated that the party's policies would be grounded in Islamic principles but that the party, whose members included women and Christians, would be nonconfessional. The party received official recognition in June, allowing it to enter candidates in upcoming elections. The Freedom and Justice Party soon achieved considerable success, winning about 47 percent of seats in elections held between November 2011 and January 2012 for the People's Assembly, the lower house of the Egyptian parliament. The ultraconservative Islamist Nūr Party came in second with around 30 percent of the seats. The strong results for Freedom and Justice and Nūr allowed Islamists to dominate the selection process for the 100-member Constituent Assembly, a body tasked with writing a new constitution.

The issue of fielding a presidential candidate arose again in March 2012 when the Muslim Brotherhood announced that Khairat al-Shater, a businessman and senior member of the organization, would run for president as the nominee of the Freedom and Justice Party, thus contradicting earlier assurances that the organization would not seek the presidency in 2012. In April 2012 Shater, who had been imprisoned under the Mubārak regime in 2008 for funding the Muslim Brotherhood,

# Ḥasan al-Bannāʿ

Ḥasan al-Bannāʿ (Oct. 14, 1906–February 12, 1949) was an Egyptian political and religious leader who established a new religious society, the Muslim Brotherhood, and played a central role in Egyptian political and social affairs.

At age 12 Ḥasan al-Bannāʿ joined the Society for Moral Behaviour, thus demonstrating at an early age the deep concern for religious affairs that characterized his entire life. In 1923 he enrolled at the Dār al-ʿUlūm, a teacher-training school in Cairo, which maintained a traditional religious and social outlook. In 1927 he was assigned to teach Arabic in a primary school in the city of Ismailia (al-Ismāʿīlīyah), near the Suez Canal, which was a focal point for the foreign economic and military occupation of Egypt. There he witnessed scenes that acutely distressed him and many other Muslims. In March 1928, with six workers from a British camp labour force, he created the Society of the Muslim Brothers (Arabic: al-Ikhwān al-Muslimūn), which aimed at a rejuvenation of Islam.

In the 1930s, at his own request, Ḥasan al-Bannāʿ was transferred to a teaching post in Cairo. By the advent of World War II the Muslim Brotherhood had grown enormously and had become a potent element on the Egyptian scene, attracting significant numbers of students, civil servants, urban labourers, and others, and representing almost every group in Egyptian society.

Many of the members came to view the Egyptian government as betraying the interests of Egyptian nationalism. For a while Ḥasan al-Bannāʿ tried to maintain a tactical alliance with the government, but he and his followers had become a threat to the central authorities. In the turmoil of the postwar years many elements of the society passed beyond his authority, and members were implicated in a number of assassinations, notably that of Prime Minister al-Nuqrāshī in December 1948. With the connivance of the government, Ḥasan al-Bannāʿ himself was assassinated the following year.

was disqualified from running by Egypt's election commission under a rule banning candidates with prior criminal convictions. Mohammed Morsi, the head of the Freedom and Justice Party, entered the race as Shater's replacement.

Morsi won the largest total in the first round of voting in May and defeated Ahmed Shafiq, a former prime minister under Mubārak, in a runoff held on June 16 and 17. Exuberance over Morsi's victory was tempered by the ongoing outcry over the June 14 ruling by the Egyptian Supreme Constitutional Court calling for the dissolution of the Muslim Brotherhood-led People's Assembly on the grounds that legislative elections held between November 2011 and January 2012 failed to follow procedures requiring that one-third of the seats be reserved for independent candidates. The Islamist-dominated Constituent Assembly remained intact.

On Nov. 30, 2012, the Constituent Assembly approved a draft constitution written by Islamists without the input of boycotting Christian and secularist members. Morsi called for a referendum on the draft to be held on December 15. Critics accused Morsi of using his power to force through a constitution favourable to the Muslim Brotherhood; crowds demanding Morsi's ouster gathered at the presidential palace and ransacked several Muslim Brotherhood offices. The draft constitution was approved by voters and took effect in late December, but anti-Morsi protests continued.

Morsi's administration faced increasingly vocal opposition in 2013, led by activists who accused the incumbents of inaction regarding Egypt's weak economy, failing public services, and deteriorating security situation. A massive protest calling for Morsi's resignation was held on June 30, 2013, the first anniversary of his inauguration.

On July 1 the head of the Egyptian armed forces, Gen. Abdel Fattah al-Sisi, issued an ultimatum declaring that the military would intervene if Morsi was unable to placate the

# Pan Am Flight 103 Disaster

Also called the Lockerbie bombing, the Pan Am Flight 103 disaster was a terrorist bombing of a passenger airliner operated by Pan American World Airways (Pan Am) on Dec. 21, 1988, that killed 270 people.

About 7:00 PM on December 21, Pan Am Flight 103, a Boeing 747 en route to New York City from London, exploded over Lockerbie, Scotland. The plane had reached a height of approximately 31,000 feet (9,500 metres) and was preparing for the oceanic portion of the flight when a timer-activated bomb detonated. The bomb, constructed with the odourless plastic explosive Semtex, was hidden in a cassette player that was stored in a suitcase. The blast broke the plane into thousands of pieces that landed in an area covering roughly 850 square miles (2,200 square km). All 259 passengers and crew members were killed. Falling wreckage destroyed 21 houses and killed an additional 11 people on the ground.

Although the passengers aboard the plane came from 21 countries, the majority of them were Americans, and the attack increased terrorism fears in the United States. Investigators believed that two Libyan intelligence agents were responsible for the bombing; many speculated that the attack had been retaliation for a 1986 U.S. bombing campaign against Libya's capital city, Tripoli. Libyan leader Muammar al-Qaddafi refused to turn over the two suspects. As a result, the United States and the United Nations Security Council imposed economic sanctions against Libya. In 1998 Qaddafi finally accepted a proposal to extradite the men. In 2001, after an investigation that involved interviewing 15,000 people and examining 180,000 pieces of evidence, Abdelbaset Ali Mohmed al-Megrahi was convicted of the bombing and sentenced to 20 (later 27) years in prison. The other man, Lamin Khalifa Fhimah, was acquitted. The Libyan government eventually agreed to pay damages to the families of the victims of the attack. In 2009 Megrahi, who had been diagnosed with terminal cancer, was released from

*Wreckage of Pan Am Flight 103 after it exploded over the town of Lockerbie, Scotland, on Dec. 21, 1988.* Bryn Colton/Hulton Archive/Getty Images

prison in Scotland on compassionate grounds and allowed to return to Libya; the United States strongly disagreed with the Scottish government's decision. In July 2010 an investigation spurred by U.S. senators revealed that oil company BP had lobbied for a prisoner transfer agreement between the United Kingdom and Libya. Although both BP and the U.K. government denied that Megrahi was discussed specifically, in 2009 British Justice Minister Jack Straw had stated that BP's business dealings with the Libyan government were a factor in considering his case.

protesters. Morsi responded by offering negotiations with the opposition but refused to step down. On July 3 the military made good on its ultimatum, suspending the constitution, removing Morsi from the presidency, and appointing a new transitional administration. Morsi and several other Muslim Brotherhood figures were placed under arrest, and television stations associated with the Muslim Brotherhood were shut down.

While Morsi's opponents celebrated, enraged supporters of the Muslim Brotherhood took to the streets to denounce the removal of a democratically elected leader. Tensions erupted into violence on July 8 when Egyptian security forces opened fire on a crowd of Muslim Brotherhood supporters outside a military base in Cairo, killing at least 50 people and wounding hundreds more.

# Tamil Tigers

The Tamil Tigers, byname of Liberation Tigers of Tamil Eelam (LTTE), is a guerrilla organization that sought to establish an independent Tamil state, Eelam, in northern and eastern Sri Lanka.

The LTTE was established in 1976 by Velupillai Prabhakaran as the successor to an organization he had formed earlier in the 1970s. The LTTE grew to become one of the world's most sophisticated and tightly organized insurgent groups. During the 1970s the organization carried out a number of guerrilla attacks. In 1983, after the killing of 13 soldiers by Tamil guerrillas and retaliatory attacks by the Sri Lankan military, large-scale violence erupted between the government and the LTTE. By 1985 the group was in control of Jaffna and most of the Jaffna Peninsula in northern Sri Lanka. Under Prabhakaran's orders, the LTTE had eliminated most of its rival Tamil groups by 1987. To fund its operations, the group engaged in illegal activities (including bank robberies and drug smuggling) and the extortion of Tamils in Sri Lanka and elsewhere, but it also received considerable voluntary financial support from Tamils living abroad.

The LTTE lost control of Jaffna in October 1987 to an Indian peacekeeping force (IPKF) that had been sent to Sri Lanka

to assist in the implementation of a complete cease-fire. However, following the withdrawal of the IPKF in March 1990, the
Tigers grew in strength and conducted several successful guerrilla operations and terrorist attacks. On May 21, 1991, a suicide bomber killed former Indian Prime Minister Rajiv Gandhi
while he was campaigning in the Indian state of Tamil Nadu.
Other attacks included an August 1992 land-mine explosion in
Jaffna, which killed 10 senior military commanders; the May
1993 assassination of Sri Lankan President Ranasinghe Prema-
dasa; a January 1996 suicide bomb attack on the central bank
of Colombo that killed 100 people; and a July 2001 attack on
Colombo's international airport that destroyed half of the
country's commercial airliners. An elite unit of the LTTE, the
"Black Tigers," was responsible for carrying out suicide attacks.
If faced with unavoidable capture by Sri Lankan authorities,
those operatives and others purportedly committed suicide by
swallowing cyanide capsules that they wore around their necks.

Negotiations between the LTTE and the government
broke down in the mid-1990s. In December 2000 the LTTE
declared a unilateral cease-fire, which lasted only until April.
Thereafter, fighting between the guerrillas and the government
again intensified until February 2002, when the government
and the LTTE signed a permanent cease-fire agreement.
Sporadic violence continued, however, and in 2006 the
European Union added the LTTE to its list of banned terrorist
organizations. Soon after, heavy fighting erupted between the
rebels and government forces, and thousands were killed.

In January 2008 the government formally abandoned
the 2002 cease-fire agreement, and authorities captured
major strongholds of the LTTE over the following months.
The town of Kilinochchi, the administrative centre of the
LTTE, came under government control in January 2009. By
late April, government troops had cornered the remaining
LTTE fighters along a small stretch of the northeast coast. A

final offensive by army forces in mid-May succeeded in over-running and occupying the rebels' last stronghold, and the LTTE leadership (including Prabhakaran) was killed. The number of civil war–related deaths in Sri Lanka since the early 1980s was estimated at between 70,000 and 80,000, with many tens of thousands more displaced by the fighting.

# Japanese Red Army

The Japanese Red Army, or the United Red Army Japanese Rengo Sekigun, was a militant Japanese organization that was formed in 1969 in the merger of two far-left factions. Beginning in 1970, the Red Army undertook several major terrorist operations, including the hijacking of several Japan Air Lines airplanes, a massacre at Tel Aviv's Lod Airport (1972), and the seizure and occupation of embassies in various countries. In 1971–72 the organization underwent severe factional infighting that led to the execution of 14 of its militants by fellow Red Army members. These killings shocked the Japanese public and were followed by successful government prosecutions of many of the perpetrators. Although the Red Army remained quite small, its terrorist activities continued into the 1990s. At the beginning of the 21st century, several members were expelled from Jordan and returned to Japan, where they were arrested.

# Moro National Liberation Front (MNLF)

The Moro National Liberation Front (MNLF) is a Muslim separatist movement in the southern Philippines that has employed guerrilla tactics and violence in its campaign for the creation of an independent, democratic Islamic state.

Taking its name from the Muslim Moro peoples of Mindanao and other southern islands of the Philippines, the MNLF led an insurgency against the Philippine government that began in 1973, soon after President Ferdinand Marcos imposed martial law. The MNLF's well-organized and sophisticated military force, known as the Bangsa Moro Army, had 30,000 fighters at the time of its greatest strength in the 1970s. In 1975 Marcos conceded that the Moros' economic grievances, at least, were justified, particularly against Christian landowners; but government offers of regional autonomy were rejected by the MNLF, which continued to demand complete independence for the Moro islands. The MNLF boycotted elections in Mindanao, giving legislative control to the National Society Movement. The organization subsequently was weakened by a series of factional splits, including breaks in the 1970s that resulted in the formation of the Moro Islamic Liberation Front (MILF) and the Bangsa Moro Liberation Organization.

Although martial law was lifted at the beginning of 1981, guerrilla activity continued. In February 1981 the MNLF attacked government forces, killing more than 120 troops on the island of Pata. In addition to violent attacks, the group also kidnapped Roman Catholic bishops, foreigners, and others and made ransom demands for their hostages.

In 1986 Marcos was forced from power by a popular revolution. The new president, Corazon Aquino, and the leader of the MNLF, Nur Misuari, quickly arranged for a cease-fire, and in January 1987 the MNLF agreed to drop its demand for an independent state in return for regional autonomy. However, the MILF refused to accept the agreement, and discussions between the government and opposition groups broke down. In 1988 the MNLF officially lifted its cease-fire. Despite the breakdown in the talks and the continued fighting, the government held referendums that led to the establishment of an autonomous region for Muslim Mindanao in 1990.

After several more years of skirmishes, Philippine President Fidel Ramos and Misuari concluded a peace accord in 1996. Later that year, Misuari was elected governor of the autonomous region. However, clashes between the MNLF and the government continued into the 21st century. During the last three decades of the 20th century, the fighting between Moro guerrilla groups and the government resulted in about 100,000 deaths.

# ETA

ETA, abbreviation of Basque Euskadi Ta Askatasuna ("Basque Homeland and Liberty"), is a Basque separatist organization in Spain that used terrorism in its campaign for an independent Basque state.

ETA grew out of the Basque Nationalist Party (Partido Nacionalista Vasco; PNV), which was founded in 1894 and which managed to survive, though illegally, under the fascist regime of Francisco Franco by maintaining its headquarters in exile in Paris and keeping quietly out of sight in Spain. In 1959 some youthful members, angered at the party's persistent rejection of armed struggle, broke away and founded ETA. During the next few years the new organization developed groupings associated increasingly with Marxist positions and set revolutionary socialism as their goal. In 1966, at ETA's fifth conference, the organization divided ideologically into two wings—the "nationalists," or ETA-V, who adhered to the traditional goal of Basque autonomy, and the "ideologists," or ETA-VI, who favoured a Marxist-Leninist brand of Basque independence and engaged in sabotage and, from 1968, assassination. The Franco regime's attempts to crush ETA in the Basque provinces were severe, involving arbitrary arrest, beatings, and torture. By 1969–70 the principal leaders had been rounded up by the police and subjected to military trials in the city of Burgos.

Factionalism plagued ETA in the 1970s and '80s, with various internal groups alternating between violence and political action. After Franco's death in 1975, Spain's democratic governments moved to establish regional autonomy for the Basque provinces and to offer pardons to ETA members who renounced terrorism. In the following decade, however, the number of ETA killings by bombing and assassination multiplied tenfold compared to the occurrences under Franco's ironhanded repression. Most of those assassinated were high-ranking Spanish military officers, judges, and government officials.

ETA came to rely financially on robberies, kidnappings, and "revolutionary taxes" extorted from businessmen. It formed political front organizations—such as Herri Batasuna, which generally was considered the political wing of ETA—to contest elections in the post-Franco period while continuing to engage in assassinations and car bombings to achieve its goals. Successive ETA leaders were captured by the Spanish government or killed in factional disputes, but the organization remained active. In 1983 two ETA members were kidnapped and murdered by Spanish security forces as part of what many considered a "dirty war" against the group. In 2000 two government officials were convicted for their role in the murders and sentenced to more than 70 years in prison.

In September 1998 ETA called a cease-fire, but it lasted only 14 months. Continued violence by ETA at the beginning of the 21st century once again led the Spanish government to attempt to suppress the organization, and in March 2006 ETA announced a permanent cease-fire. In December 2006, however, ETA members carried out a bombing at Madrid's international airport that killed two people, and in June 2007 it officially lifted its cease-fire. Although increased policing efforts and the arrests of several high-ranking ETA leaders in subsequent years weakened the organization, violent attacks continued. Bombings occurred in the city of Burgos and on the island of Majorca in

July 2009, less than a month before the 50th anniversary of ETA's founding. In 2010, however, the organization announced that it would not carry out "armed actions." The cease-fire was dismissed by the Spanish government, which called for ETA to renounce violence and to disarm. In October 2011 a conference was held to discuss the conflict, and the attendees, who included former UN Secretary-General Kofi Annan and Sinn Féin leader Gerry Adams, urged ETA to renounce violence and called on France and Spain to open talks. Shortly thereafter ETA declared the definite cessation of its armed activities, though it vowed to continue to seek an independent Basque state.

# Red Brigades

The Red Brigades, or the Italian Brigate Rosse, was a militant left-wing organization in Italy that gained notoriety in the 1970s for kidnappings, murders, and sabotage. Its self-proclaimed aim was to undermine the Italian state and pave the way for a Marxist upheaval led by a "revolutionary proletariat."

The reputed founder of the Red Brigades was Renato Curcio, who in 1967 set up a leftist study group at the University of Trento dedicated to figures such as Karl Marx, Mao Zedong, and Che Guevara. In 1969 Curcio married a fellow radical, Margherita Cagol, and moved with her to Milan, where they attracted a coterie of followers. Proclaiming the existence of the Red Brigades in November 1970 through the firebombing of various factories and warehouses in Milan, the group began kidnapping the following year and in 1974 committed its first assassination; among its victims that year was the chief inspector of Turin's antiterrorist squad.

Despite the arrest and imprisonment of hundreds of alleged terrorists throughout the country—including Curcio himself in 1976—the random assassinations continued. In 1978 the Red Brigades kidnapped and murdered former Prime

Minister Aldo Moro. In December 1981 a U.S. Army officer with the North Atlantic Treaty Organization (NATO), Brigadier General James Dozier, was abducted and held captive by the Red Brigades for 42 days before Italian police rescued him unharmed from a hideout in Padua. Between 1974 and 1988, the Red Brigades carried out about 50 attacks, in which nearly 50 people were killed. A common nonlethal tactic employed by the group was "kneecapping," in which a victim was shot in the knees so that he could not walk again.

At its height in the 1970s, the Red Brigades was believed to comprise 400 to 500 full-time members, 1,000 members who helped periodically, and a few thousand supporters who provided funds and shelter. Careful, systematic police work led to the arrest and imprisonment of many of the Red Brigades' leaders and ordinary members from the mid-1970s onward, and by the late 1980s the organization was all but destroyed. However, a group claiming to be the Red Brigades took responsibility in the 1990s for various violent attacks, including those against a senior Italian government adviser, a U.S. base in Aviano, and the NATO Defense College.

# Red Army Faction (RAF)

The Red Army Faction (RAF), byname Baader-Meinhof Gang, was a West German radical leftist group formed in 1968 and popularly named after two of its early leaders, Andreas Baader (1943–77) and Ulrike Meinhof (1934–76).

From its early years, members of the Red Army Faction supported themselves through bank robberies and engaged in terrorist bombings and arson, especially of West German corporations and businesses and of West German and U.S. military installations in West Germany. They also kidnapped and assassinated prominent political and business figures. By the mid-1970s, the group expanded its scope outside West Germany and occasionally allied itself with militant Palestinian groups. For example, in 1976 two Baader-Meinhof guerrillas took part in a Palestinian hijacking of an Air France jetliner, which eventually ended after the successful Entebbe raid in Uganda by Israeli commandos.

The Red Army Faction included at least 22 core members in the early 1970s, most of whom, including Meinhof, had been jailed by the summer of 1972. Baader, escaping one imprisonment in 1970, was arrested again in 1976. Meinhof hanged herself in her cell in 1976. Three others, including Baader, were found shot dead in their cells on October 18, 1977. Ostensibly suicides, their deaths came one day after West German commandos stormed a hijacked Lufthansa plane in Mogadishu, Somalia, blocking the hijackers' attempt to win the release of their jailed comrades as ransom for their hostages. Thereafter, the Red Army Faction continued its terrorist activities and splintered into a number of groups.

After the collapse of the communist government in East Germany in 1989–90, it was discovered that the Red Army Faction had been given training, shelter, and supplies by the Stasi, the secret police of the former communist regime. Greatly weakened by the demise of communism throughout eastern Europe, the group announced an end to its terrorist campaign in 1992, and several of its surviving militants were arrested and tried. However, it retained a following among some European radicals, and in 1996 several thousand sympathizers attended a meeting to commemorate the anniversary of Meinhof's death. The group formally disbanded in 1998, though arrests and trials continued.

# Boston Marathon Bombing of 2013

The Boston Marathon bombing terrorist attack took place a short distance from the finish line of the Boston Marathon on April 15, 2013. A pair of homemade bombs detonated in the crowd watching the race, killing three people and injuring more than 260.

The explosions occurred roughly five hours into the 117th running of the Boston Marathon. The marathon is traditionally held on Patriots' Day, a public holiday in Massachusetts, and the festive atmosphere draws hundreds of thousands of spectators to the 26.2-mile (42-km) route from Hopkinton, Mass., to Boston's Back Bay neighbourhood. At approximately 2:50 PM, the first bomb exploded less than half a block from the race's finish line, on the north side of Boylston Street. Roughly 12 seconds later, a second bomb exploded some 600 feet (180 meters) from the first. It too was planted on the north side of Boylston Street amid a crowd of onlookers. First responders reacted immediately, and a medical tent that had been erected to treat runners was turned into an emergency medical facility. Three bombing victims died of their injuries, and more than 100 of the seriously injured were transferred to area hospitals as local police and federal investigators surveyed a crime scene that covered 15 square blocks.

In the days following the attacks, law-enforcement personnel solicited assistance from the public, asking for photographs or video footage that might prove relevant to their investigation. It was revealed that devices used in the attacks were pressure cookers that had been packed with an explosive substance, nails, and ball bearings—the latter two elements acting as shrapnel when the bombs

*Seventy-eight-year-old marathoner Bill Iffrig on the ground after a second explosion near the finish line of the 117th Boston Marathon on April 15, 2013.* Boston Globe/Getty Images

detonated. On April 18 the Federal Bureau of Investigation released images and video of two men identified as suspects in the attacks, including one photograph that showed one of the men placing a package at the location of the second explosion.

Within hours, the fatal shooting of a Massachusetts Institute of Technology campus police officer and the armed carjacking of a sport-utility vehicle in Cambridge, Mass., spurred speculation about a possible connection between these crimes and the marathon bombings. Police pursued the stolen vehicle to the Boston suburb of Watertown, and an intense firefight ensued, during which Tamerlan Tsarnaev, identified as one of the two suspects in the bombing, was wounded by explosives and multiple gunshots and died. His younger brother, Dzhokhar Tsarnaev, fled the scene, triggering a massive house-to-house manhunt on April 19 that covered the surrounding area and resulted in much of Greater Boston coming to an unprecedented standstill as officials requested that residents remain in their homes and that businesses not open. The "stay home" order was lifted at 6:00 PM, and later that evening Tsarnaev—who had concealed himself in a boat in a residential backyard—was located and apprehended by police. On April 22 federal prosecutors charged Tsarnaev with using a weapon of mass destruction in the marathon attacks; if convicted, he faced the possibility of the death penalty.

# FALN

FALN, abbreviation of Spanish Fuerzas Armadas de Liberación Nacional ("Armed Forces of National Liberation"), was a separatist organization in Puerto Rico that has used violence in its campaign for Puerto Rican independence from the United States.

Although not formed until about 1974, the FALN had antecedents that can be traced to the 1930s, when the violent Nationalist Party under Pedro Albizu Campos provoked riots, assassinations, and other acts of protest and bloodshed.

# Timothy McVeigh

Timothy James McVeigh (April 23, 1968–June 11, 2001), was an American militant who carried out the Oklahoma City bombing on April 19, 1995. The explosion, which killed 168 people, was the deadliest terrorist incident on U.S. soil, until the September 11 attacks in 2001.

McVeigh was the middle child in a blue-collar family in rural New York State, and he expressed an interest in guns from an early age. He graduated from high school in June 1986 and spent a short period at a local business college. Around this time he first read *The Turner Diaries* (1978), an antigovernment, neo-Nazi tract written by William Pierce. The book, which details the truck-bombing of the Washington, D.C., headquarters of the Federal Bureau of Investigation (FBI), fueled McVeigh's paranoia about a government plot to repeal the Second Amendment of the U.S. Constitution, which guarantees the right "to keep and bear arms." He enlisted in the U.S. Army in 1988 and proved to be a model soldier, earning a Bronze Star for bravery in the Persian Gulf War (1990–91). He was a candidate for the Special Forces but dropped out of the program after only two days. The experience soured him on the military, and he took an early discharge and left the army in late 1991.

McVeigh returned to New York but was unable to find steady work. He reunited with Terry Nichols and Michael Fortier, friends from his days in the army, and sold guns at fairs throughout the United States. In March 1993 he drove to Waco, Tex., to observe the ongoing FBI siege of the Branch Davidian compound. He viewed the U.S. government's actions there as illegal, and it was during this time that McVeigh, Nichols, and Fortier made contact with members of militia groups in the Midwest. In September 1994 McVeigh began actively plotting to destroy the Alfred P. Murrah Federal Building in Oklahoma City. Over the next six months, McVeigh and Nichols planned the bombing and acquired several tons of ammonium nitrate fertilizer, which, combined with fuel oil, would provide the explosive power for the bomb.

On April 19, 1995, the second anniversary of the deadly fire that ended the Branch Davidian siege, McVeigh parked the truck containing the bomb in front of the Murrah Building.

At 9:02 AM, the bomb went off, tearing off the front of the building, killing 168 people, and injuring more than 500. Slightly more than an hour later, McVeigh, driving a getaway car that he and Nichols had placed a few days earlier, was pulled over by a Oklahoma state police officer for a license plate violation. When the officer discovered that McVeigh was illegally carrying a concealed handgun, McVeigh was arrested and held in jail, pending a trial on the gun charge. While he was in custody, McVeigh was identified as "John Doe No. 1," the primary suspect in the Oklahoma City bombing. Two days after the bombing, McVeigh was taken into federal custody, and Nichols turned himself in to authorities. The two were indicted in August 1995, and Attorney Gen. Janet Reno stated that the government would seek the death penalty against both. McVeigh's month-long trial began in April 1997, and Fortier testified against him as part of a plea agreement. It took the jury three days to reach a unanimous guilty verdict. McVeigh was sentenced to death on June 13, 1997. Later that year, Terry Nichols was found guilty of conspiracy and eight counts of involuntary manslaughter and was sentenced to life in prison. On June 11, 2001, McVeigh became the first federal prisoner to be executed since 1963.

In Washington, D.C., on Nov. 1, 1950, Puerto Rican nationalists tried but failed to assassinate Pres. Harry S. Truman. On March 1, 1954, another militant Puerto Rican group sprayed gunfire into the chambers of the U.S. House of Representatives, wounding five congressmen. In 1971 bombs were set off in San Juan and other Puerto Rican cities.

The FALN first surfaced on Oct. 26, 1974, when five large bombs exploded in Manhattan—in the Wall Street area, in Rockefeller Center, and on Park Avenue—causing considerable property damage but no injuries. The FALN claimed responsibility for these acts, as it did later for bombings in Puerto Rico. Throughout the following year, the FALN boasted of a series of bombings, beginning on January 24 with a Wall Street explosion that killed four people and injured more than 50 and climaxing on October 27 with nine nearly simultaneous explosions in New York City, Washington, and Chicago that produced only property damage. Bombings continued sporadically thereafter.

In April 1980, 11 FALN members were arrested in Evanston, Ill., on charges including robbery, conspiracy, and weapons violations; they were convicted in both state and federal courts and sentenced to prison terms of as long as 90 years. Amid political controversy and over the objections of the Federal Bureau of Investigation, in 1999 Pres. Bill Clinton granted clemency to 14 convicted FALN members—none of whom had been involved in the bombings—claiming that their sentences were disproportionate to the crimes. Of the 14, 11, including eight of those involved in the 1980 robbery and three others convicted of conspiracy and other charges in 1985, were released from prison; one, who had been sentenced in 1989 to 55 years in prison for bank robbery, was scheduled to be released in five years; and two, who already had served prison terms for bank robbery, were granted waivers of their fines.

# Shining Path

The Shining Path, a Peruvian revolutionary organization that endorsed Maoism and employed guerrilla tactics and violent terrorism, was founded in 1970 in a multiple split in the Communist Party of Peru. It took its name from the maxim of the founder of Peru's first communist party, José Carlos Mariátegui: "El Marxismo-Leninismo abrirá el sendero luminoso hacia la revolución" ("Marxism-Leninism will open the shining path to revolution"). The leader and principal founder was Abimael Guzmán Reynoso, alias Comrade Gonzalo, a long-time communist and former philosophy teacher (1962–78) at the National University of San Cristóbal de Huamanga, in the city of Ayacucho in the high Andes Mountains. He and his followers, known as Senderistas, sought to restore the "pure" ideology of Mao Zedong and adopted China's Cultural Revolution as a model for their own revolutionary movement. The organization's other models were Stalinist Russia and the Khmer Rouge regime in Cambodia. Envisioning revolution as a long military offensive, the Shining Path relied primarily on the peasantry and made ruthless use of terror and violence.

With a following of young intellectuals he gathered in Ayacucho in the 1960s, Guzmán spent the next decade recruiting armed supporters among the indigenous peoples in the countryside and the poorer urban districts. The Shining Path began its revolutionary campaign in remote areas of the Andes (the group's first act of violence occurred on May 17, 1980, near Ayacucho) and soon was engaged in bombings and assassinations and other terrorist acts in various urban centres, including Lima and Callao. It gained control of poor rural and urban districts in central and southern Peru by violence and intimidation, while attracting sympathizers and supporters through its tight discipline, its organizing ability, and its emphasis on empowering the native population at the expense of Peru's traditional Spanish-speaking elite. It reportedly established cocaine-processing plants in the Huallaga valley to fund its activities.

Guzmán, whose organizational and tactical abilities underlay the Shining Path's success, was captured in a police raid in Lima on Sept. 12, 1992, and in October he was sentenced to life imprisonment on terrorism charges. Despite his conviction, the organization continued to clash with the government throughout the 1990s. In July 1999 its new leader, Oscar Ramirez Durand (alias Comrade Feliciano), was captured and, like Guzmán, sentenced to life imprisonment. In 2003 Peru's Truth and Reconciliation Committee issued a report that estimated some 70,000 people had been killed by Shining Path guerillas and government forces during the last two decades of the 20th century. The Shining Path's terrorist activities also seriously disrupted the country's economy.

# Tupamaro

Tupamaro was an Uruguayan leftist urban guerrilla organization founded in about 1963. The group was named for Túpac Amaru II, the leader of an 18th-century revolt against Spanish rule in Peru.

The chief founder of Tupamaro was Raúl Sendic, a labour organizer. The earliest Tupamaro efforts were a mixture of idealism, public relations, and theft—robbing banks and businesses and distributing food and goods to the poor. In 1968 Tupamaro began more-aggressive efforts to undermine the established order, including raids on arsenals, arson, political kidnappings (with those taken held in a secret "People's Prison"), and assassinations of a number of police officers and some others. The organization also carried out bombings against foreign interests, particularly those of Brazil and the United States. In 1971 it kidnapped the British ambassador and held him for eight months. Its success was brief, however; by the time of the June 1973 military coup in Uruguay, Tupamaro had been neutralized by government troops, which managed to kill some 300 members and imprison nearly 3,000 others. After democratic rule returned to Uruguay in 1985, most of those jailed, including Sendic, were released under a general amnesty, and Tupamaro was reorganized as a legal political party.

# CONCLUSION

Anarchy, revolution, and terrorism are not political systems but rather reactions against political systems. Anarchists distrust centralized authorities and often seek to disrupt their operation through a combination of violent and nonviolent acts. Revolutionaries seek to overthrow the established government and will often begin by using guerrilla war tactics to give a relatively small force a chance to defeat a superior military force. Terrorists use violent acts to shock and intimidate, in pursuit of political goals that may be as specific as a policy change or as broad as regime change.

There is some overlap among the three, and all have their shortcomings. Anarchism has declined as a political movement in part because its fundamental rejection of a strong central organization makes it difficult for the movement to work toward coordinated objectives. By taking on the powers that be, revolution and terrorism are somewhat long-shot propositions to begin with—they are generally based on the premise of having to operate with inferior numbers, something that tactics alone cannot always overcome. Often, the tactics themselves can become part of the downfall of revolutionary methods such as guerrilla warfare and terrorism, as excessive violence can cause them to lose the popular support necessary for their success.

Still, revolution, terrorism, and even anarchism remain part of the 21st century's socio-political landscape. It is doubtful that any of these means of radical change appeal to the majority of people around the world, but as long as political and economic systems alienate even a minority of their citizens, some of those minorities will look for extreme measures that can act as a catalyst for change.

# GLOSSARY

**al-Qaeda** A broad-based militant Islamist organization founded by Osama bin Laden in the late 1980s and responsible for some of the most high-profile terrorist acts in history, including the attacks of Sept. 11, 2001.

**anarcha-feminism** A school of thought that applies anarchist principles to assessing women's role in society, since oppression of women is often a function of hierarchical orders in society.

**anarchist communism** A social system in which private property and unequal incomes would be replaced by a free distribution of goods and services.

**anarchy** Absence or denial of any authority or established order.

**civil disobedience** The refusal to obey governmental demands or commands especially as a nonviolent and usually collective means of forcing concessions from the government.

**Cold War** A conflict or dispute between two groups that does not involve actual fighting; this term generally refers to the rivalry between the United States and the U.S.S.R. from 1945 to 1991.

**collectivism** Any of several types of social organization in which the individual is seen as being subordinate to the greater society.

**commando** A military unit trained and organized as shock troops, especially for hit-and-run raids into enemy territory.

**Digger movement** A seventeenth-century movement in England that called upon people to collectively farm common lands as an alternative to private property ownership.

**direct action** Coordinated activities such as a boycott or strike designed to win concessions from parties affected by the action.

**ecoterrorism** Acts of environmental destruction committed to further a political or military objective, or disruptive acts intended to interfere with activities believed to be harmful to the environment.

**establishment terrorism** Terrorist techniques employed by a government or people within government with the goal of discouraging opposition.

**federalism** A system of government where the power sits in a series of localized bodies rather than with a centralized authority.

**fellow traveler** Someone who shares the opinions and beliefs of the people in a group or organization but does not belong to that group or organization.

**general strike** An organized refusal to work coordinated across multiple industries in order to cause the maximum amount of economic disruption.

**guerrilla warfare** Unconventional battle tactics featuring quick strikes by small groups, generally against a superior force.

**Industrial Workers of the World** An American labour union of the early 20th century dedicated to gaining control of the means of production by the workers.

**Irish Republican Army** A long-standing paramilitary organization dedicated to ending British presence in Ireland and restoring the island to one single nation.

**jihad** A holy war waged on behalf of Islam as a religious duty.

**Marxism** A theory and practice of socialism advocated by Karl Marx that included the labour theory of value, dialectical materialism, the class struggle, and dictatorship of the proletariat until the establishment of a classless society.

**mujahideen** Islamic resistance fighters who carried out a prolonged guerrilla war against Soviet occupation of Afghanistan in the 1980s.

**Mutualism** An economic system based on equal sharing of property and efforts.

**passive resistance** Resistance, especially to a government or an occupying power, characterized mainly by noncooperation.

**proletariat** The class of industrial workers who lack their own means of production and hence sell their labour to live.

**propaganda of the deed** Dramatic actions such as bombings or assassinations designed to publicize a cause.

**Reign of Terror** A period of the French Revolution that was conspicuous for mass executions of suspected enemies of the Revolution.

**revolutionary terrorism** The use of violence to generate fear in the hopes of abolishing the ruling political system in favour of new leadership.

**secular humanism** Humanism viewed as a system of values and beliefs that are opposed to the values and beliefs of traditional religions.

**social contract** An actual or hypothetical agreement among the members of an organized society or between a community and its ruler that defines and limits the rights and duties of each.

**state-sponsored terrorism** Another term for establishment terrorism.

**subrevolutionary terrorism** The use of terrorist tactics to modify the existing sociopolitical structure rather than to overthrow the ruling regime.

**suicide bombing** An extreme terrorist technique in which a person detonates an explosive device he or she is carrying.

**syndicalism** A revolutionary doctrine by which workers seize control of the economy and the government by direct means.

**Taliban** A puritanical Islamic group that ruled Afghanistan from the mid-1990s until late 2001.

**terrorism** The systematic use of violence to create a general climate of fear in a population and thereby bring about a particular political objective.

**Wobblies** A nickname for the Industrial Workers of the World.

# BIBLIOGRAPHY

## Anarchism

The best general accounts of anarchism are Peter Marshall, *Demanding the Impossible: A History of Anarchism* (1992); James Joll, *The Anarchists*, 2nd ed. (1980); Paul Avrich, *Anarchist Portraits* (1988); George Woodcock, *Anarchism*, new ed. (1986); Harold Barclay, *People Without Government*, completely rev. ed. (1990); Daniel Guérin, *Anarchism: From Theory to Practice* (1970; originally published in French, 1965); Paul Eltzbacher, *Anarchism* (1960, reprinted 1972; originally published in German, 1900); and Richard D. Sonn, *Anarchism* (1992).

Good anthologies of anarchist theory include Irving Louis Horowitz (ed.), *The Anarchists* (1964); Leonard I. Krimerman and Lewis Perry (eds.), *Patterns of Anarchy* (1966); and David E. Apter and James Joll (eds.), *Anarchism Today* (1971).

For a comprehensive bibliography of anarchist literature from different countries over the last two centuries, see Denise Fauvel-Rouif (ed.), *Anarchism* (1982); and Helene Strub (ed.), *Anarchism*, vol. 2 (1993). There are also useful selected bibliographies in all the books listed above.

The earliest formulations of modern anarchist thought can be found in William Godwin, *An Enquiry Concerning Political Justice and Its Influence on General Virtue and Happiness*, 2 vol. (1792). Pierre-Joseph Proudhon's key anarchist work is *Qu'est-ce que la propriété?* (1840; *What Is Property?*, trans. by Benjamin R. Tucker, 1876). Of Peter Kropotkin's many writings, his *Memoirs of a Revolutionist* (1899) is essential. See also his *La conquête du pain* (1892; *The Conquest of Bread*, 1906), *Fields, Factories, and Workshops* (1899), and *Mutual Aid: A Factor of Evolution* (1902). Leo Tolstoy's Christian anarchist concepts can be found in many of his later works, including *T Sarstvo Bozhie vnutri nas* (1894; *The Kingdom of God Is Within You*, trans. by Constance Garnett, 1894), and *V chem moîa vera* (1884; *What I Believe*, trans. by Constantine Popoff, 1885). Emma Goldman's voluminous writings include her autobiography, *Living My Life*, 2 vol. (1931, reissued 1988); see also the autobiography of Goldman's comrade Alexander Berkman, *Prison Memoirs of an Anarchist* (1912, reprinted 1970).

For an analysis of Godwin's work, see Isaac Kramnick, *The Politics of Political Philosophy, A Case Study: Godwin's Anarchism and Radical England* (1970). For information on Proudhon's life and thought, see Stewart Edwards (ed.), *Selected Writings of Pierre-Joseph Proudhon* (1969); K. Steven Vincent, *Pierre-Joseph Proudhon and the Rise of French Republican Socialism* (1984); Alan Ritter, *The Political Thought of Pierre-Joseph Proudhon* (1969, reprinted 1980); and Robert L. Hoffman, *Revolutionary Justice: The Social and Political Theory of P.-J. Proudhon* (1972). For an anthology of Kropotkin's writings, see Martin A. Miller (ed.), *Peter Kropotkin: Selected Writings on Anarchism and Revolution* (1970). On Kropotkin's life, consult Martin A. Miller, *Kropotkin* (1976); Caroline Cahm, *Kropotkin and the Rise of Revolutionary Anarchism, 1872–1886* (1989); and George Woodcock and Ivan Avakumovic, *The Anarchist Prince: A Biographical Study of Peter Kropotkin* (1950, reissued 1970). Two convenient volumes that explore the anarchist ideas of Michael Bakunin are Arthur Lehning (ed.), *Selected Writings [of] Michael Bakunin* (1973); and Sam Dolgoff (ed.), *Bakunin on Anarchism*, 2nd rev. ed. (1980; originally published as *Bakunin on Anarchy*, 1972). For biographies of Bakunin, see Edward H. Carr, *Michael Bakunin* (1937, reissued 1975); Arthur P. Mendel, *Michael Bakunin: Roots of Apocalypse* (1981); and Eugene Pyziur, *The Doctrine of Anarchism of Michael A. Bakunin* (1955, reissued 1968).

Articles by Emma Goldman are collected in her *Anarchism and Other Essays*, 3rd rev. ed. (1917, reprinted 1967); and in

Alix Kates Shulman (ed.), *Red Emma Speaks*, 3rd ed. (1996). For a sympathetic biography of Goldman, see Richard Drinnon, *Rebel in Paradise* (1961, reissued 1982). The correspondence of Goldman and Berkman can be found in Richard Drinnon and Anna Maria Drinnon (eds.), *Nowhere at Home* (1975). The life of Johann Most is studied in Frederic Trautmann, *The Voice of Terror: A Biography of Johann Most* (1980).

The best general account of the anarchist movement in Russia remains Paul Avrich, *The Russian Anarchists* (1967, reprinted 1980). For documents on the anarchist critique of Lenin and Bolshevism, see Paul Avrich (ed.), *Anarchists in the Russian Revolution* (1973). Voline, *The Unknown Revolution, 1917–1921* (1955; originally published in French, 1947), is a good anarchist memoir of the Russian Revolution.

On the origins and history of American individualist anarchism, see Carlotta R. Anderson, *All-American Anarchist: Joseph A. Labadie and the Labor Movement* (1998); James J. Martin, *Men Against the State: The Expositors of Individualist Anarchism in America, 1827–1908* (1953, reissued 1970); and Rudolf Rocker, *Pioneers of American Freedom*, trans. from German (1949). An excellent collection of historical source material can be found in Paul Avrich, *Anarchist Voices: An Oral History of Anarchism in America* (1995). There is a large literature on Haymarket. Especially useful are Paul Avrich, *The Haymarket Tragedy* (1984); and David Roediger and Franklin Rosemont (eds.), *Haymarket Scrapbook* (1986). Anarchist influences in the Industrial Workers of the World are discussed in Salvatore Salerno, *Red November, Black November: Culture and Community in the Industrial Workers of the World* (1989).

P. Holgate, *Malatesta* (1956), is a study of the leading Italian anarchist. See also Vernon Richards (ed.), *Errico Malatesta: His Life & Ideas*, 3rd ed. (1984). On France, see Marie Fleming, *The Anarchist Way to Socialism: Elisée Reclus and Nineteenth-Century European Anarchism* (1979). On Germany, the best book is

Andrew R. Carlson, *Anarchism in Germany* (1972). See also Eugene Lunn, *Prophet of Community: The Romantic Socialism of Gustav Landauer* (1973). On Spain, see Temma Kaplan, *Anarchists of Andalusia* (1977); and Robert W. Kern, *Red Years/Black Years: A Political History of Spanish Anarchism, 1911–1937* (1978). For developments in England, see Hermia Oliver, *The International Anarchist Movement in Late Victorian London* (1983).

Arif Dirlik, *Anarchism in the Chinese Revolution* (1991), is a comprehensive analysis of anarchism in China during the first three decades of the 20th century. Ming K. Chan and Arif Dirlik, *Schools into Fields and Factories: Anarchists, the Guomindang, and the National Labor University in Shanghai, 1927–1932* (1991), is a wide-ranging study of an educational experiment in which anarchists played a leading role. Edward S. Krebs, *Shifu: Soul of Chinese Anarchism* (1998), is a detailed if somewhat hagiographic biography of the most revered of Chinese anarchists. Olga Lang, *Pa Chin and His Writings: Chinese Youth Between the Two Revolutions* (1967), is a thorough treatment of the anarchist writer. Peter Zarrow, *Anarchism and Chinese Political Culture* (1990), which focuses on anarchist activity in the 1910s, is especially strong on anarchist contributions to feminist issues.

English-language studies of anarchism in Japan have concentrated largely on individuals. Major works are John Crump, *Hatta Shuzo and Pure Anarchism in Interwar Japan* (1993); F.G. Notehelfer, *Kotoku Shusui: Portrait of a Japanese Radical* (1971); and Thomas A. Stanley, *Osugi Sakae, Anarchist in Taisho Japan: The Creativity of the Ego* (1982). A translation of Osugi's autobiography is available in English as *The Autobiography of Osugi Sakae*, trans. with annotations by Byron K. Marshall (1992).

A good discussion of anarchism in Vietnam is Hue-tam Ho Tai, *Radicalism and the Origins of the Vietnamese Revolution* (1992).

Anarchist influences in early 20th-century American art are discussed in Alan Antliff, *Anarchist Modernism: Art, Politics, and the First American Avant-Garde* (2001). Richard Porton, *Film and the Anarchist Imagination* (1999), examines anarchist films as well as anarchist elements in mainstream films. Ron Sakolsky and Fred Wei-han Ho (eds.), *Sounding Off! Music as Subversion/Resistance/Revolution* (1995), includes much anarchist material. Ron Sakolsky (ed.), *Surrealist Subversions* (2001), focuses on anarchist elements in Surrealism.

Daniel Cohn-Bendit and Gabriel Cohn-Bendit, *Obsolete Communism* (1968; originally published in French, 1968), by two participants in the 1968 student uprisings in Paris, effectively describes anarchist involvement in the protests; its critique of the contemporary French Communist Party is richly informed by a historical analysis of early anarchist resistance to Bolshevism in Russia. David Apter and James Joll (eds.), *Anarchism Today* (1971), is a very good summation of the influence of anarchism around the world in the aftermath of the student uprisings of the 1960s. Noam Chomsky, *Radical Priorities*, 2nd rev. ed., edited by Carlos P. Otero (1984), includes a good sample of Chomsky's anarchism-related writings. Margaret S. Marsh, *Anarchist Women, 1870–1920* (1981), treats the early development of feminist anarchism. Essays on contemporary anarchafeminism by Elaine Leeder, Susan Brown, Peggy Kornegger, and Carol Erlich appear in Howard J. Ehrlich (ed.), *Reinventing Anarchy, Again* (1996). The most influential thinking in contemporary anarchism can be found in the work of Murray Bookchin, *Post-Scarcity Anarchism*, 2nd ed. (1986), and *The Modern Crisis*, 2nd rev. ed. (1987).

# Revolution

Bernard Bailyn, *The Ideological Origins of the American Revolution*, enlarged ed. (1992), examines the transmission of English republican ideology and its American reception. John Richard Alden, *The American Revolution, 1775–1783* (1954, reissued 1987), is distinguished for its political and military analyses. Jack P. Greene (ed.), *The American Revolution: Its Character and Limits* (1987), contains a valuable collection of essays. Robert Middlekauff, *The Glorious Cause: The American Revolution, 1763–1789* (1982, reprinted 1985), examines the revolution from a somewhat older point of view than is now fashionable. Piers Mackesy, *The War for America, 1775–1783* (1964, reissued 1993), explains the British side of the war. J.G.A. Pocock (ed.), *Three British Revolutions: 1641, 1688, 1776* (1980), sets the American Revolution in the historical context of British experience. Military histories include John Shy, *Toward Lexington: The Role of the British Army in the Coming of the American Revolution* (1965), on the British army in America; Don Higginbotham, *The War of American Independence: Military Attitudes, Policies, and Practice, 1763–1789* (1971, reprinted 1983), which shows the interrelationship of military and political developments; Charles Royster, *A Revolutionary People at War: The Continental Army and American Character, 1775–1783* (1979, reissued 1986); and William M. Fowler, Jr., *Rebels Under Sail* (1976), on the American navy. Stephen R. Platt, *Autumn in the Heavenly Kingdom: China, the West, and the Epic Story of the Taiping Civil War* (2012); Jonathan D. Spence, *God's Chinese Son: The Taiping Heavenly Kingdom of Hong Xiuquan* (1996).

Jeremy D. Popkin, *A Short History of the French Revolution*, 2nd ed. (1998), is a brief overview of the event with bibliography. William Doyle, *The Oxford History of the French Revolution* (1989, reprinted 1992); and David Andress, *French Society in Revolution, 1789–1799* (1999) are more detailed studies. Samuel F. Scott and Barry Rothaus (eds.), *Historical Dictionary of the French Revolution 1789–1799*, 2 vol. (1985), is a reliable source.

# Terrorism

A collection of critical essays on various international movements and crises is Martha Crenshaw (ed.), *Terrorism in Context* (1995). A comprehensive survey of patterns of terrorism is Bruce Hoffman, *Inside Terrorism* (1999). Mark Juergensmeyer, *Terror in the Mind of God: The Global Rise of Religion's Violence* (2000), studies the relationship between religion and political violence. The relationship between politics and terrorism is explored in Grant Wardlaw, *Political Terrorism: Theory, Tactics, and Counter-Measures*, 2nd ed., rev. and extended (1989); and Paul Wilkinson, *Terrorism and the Liberal State*, 2nd ed., rev., extended, and updated (1986). Works examining trends in terrorism in the 1990s include Walter Laqueur, *The New Terrorism: Fanaticism and the Arms of Mass Destruction* (1999); and Richard A. Falkenrath, Robert D. Newman, and Bradley A. Thayer, *America's Achilles' Heel: Nuclear, Biological, and Chemical Terrorism and Covert Attack* (1998).

# INDEX